See Ya' Further Up the Creek

A Collection of Stories and Poems

By
Homer C. Ledford

Illustrated by
Cindy (Ledford) Lowy
Poetry contributions by
Cindy Lowy, Colista Ledford,
Julia (Ledford) Baker, Mark L. Ledford,
and Mattie (Ledford) Conkwright

With Foreword
by
Loyal Jones

For my wonderful wife, Colista, and children,
Mark, Cindy, Julia, and Mattie Lee

Cover illustration by Cindy (Ledford) Lowy
Cover layout and design by Dan Baker
Selected photography by William H. Johnson
Publication production by Walter A. Johnson, Jr.

Kentucky Traditions Publishing
125 Sunset Heights
Winchester, Kentucky 40391

Contents

Continued

3

Contents continued

Foreword

Homer Ledford and I have been friends for more than fifty years. We met at the John C. Campbell Folk School in Brasstown, North Carolina. Homer was an authentic student there, and I was a local hanger-on. Homer was even then an accomplished storyteller and musician. He had first seen dulcimers at the Folk School (hanging on the walls as decoration) and, with his lively interest in everything, started to build some. I had somehow gotten the notion that I could learn to play the fiddle and I got Homer to teach me a tune or two. From his look, I think he concluded that I must have been hiding behind the door when musical talent was handed out, but he was too kind to say so. That's how we met.

Homer aspired to a college education, and he left in 1949 for Berea College. I looked around one day and found that all my friends had gone off somewhere to better themselves, and so I, too, decided to go to college. I figured that if Berea College was good enough for Homer, it was good enough for me, and so I joined him there. Berea College is a work-your-way through type of school, and Homer had gotten a job in the college's Woodcraft Industry where he carved animals for sale in the gift shop. Since I had done a little carving at Brasstown, I signed up there also. Homer and I laughed over the poetic surnames of our fellow workers: Payne, Peace, Outlaw, and Angel. We had a wonderful time in Woodcraft, telling tales and playing tricks and practical jokes on each other, and carving improbable animals along with a few the college could actually sell. We got 25 cents for each one. On the side, Homer was doing some really first-rate carvings of birds and pins and making dulcimers. He was one of the best wood craftsmen I ever saw. When my mother sent my fiddle, and it got busted in the mail, Homer helped me to take off the top, splice and repair it and glue it back on again. In the evenings we gathered in Homer's room and picked and fiddled and sang. Marvin Carroll, who later was to join Homer's Bluegrass band, was there, along with the college violin teacher who cautioned us not to tell his musical colleagues.

Homer's real interest was in woodworking, and Berea didn't offer an industrial program at the time. Instead he studied economics and business. When he learned of the fine Industrial Arts Program at Eastern Kentucky University, he transferred there to graduate. However, we remained friends, and when he and his Berea classmate Colista Spradlin decided to get married, I served as his best man, or as Homer put it, "He shoved me through the door."

We've also kept in touch through the years when Homer developed into one of the great wood craftsmen, making dulcimers (6000), banjos *(525)*, guitars (36), mandolins (36), a few innovative instruments and several weird contraptions that he plays for comic effect. Homer is so good at what he does that folklorist Gerald Alvey published a scholarly book about him, *Dulcimer Maker: The Craft of Homer Ledford,* now in it's second edition (University Press of Kentucky). A television documentary: *Homer Ledford: Instrument Maker,* has been produced by Stan Petrey of *Timberwolf Productions, Inc.,* Lexington, Kentucky, and aired by Kentucky Education Television. His instruments are exhibited in the Smithsonian Institution, as well as in the hands of many people.

Homer has also put together one of the best Old-Time-Bluegrass groups in the country, the Cabin Creek Band, that he writes about in this book. Of course Homer is the artistic leader, superb instrumentalist, and spokesman for this outfit. However, his singing is about like my fiddling, but he's had the good sense to get Rollie Carpenter, Pam Case, and L.C. Johnson to do the singing, and Marvin Carroll to do the fiddling, and they have such a wonderful old-timey, nostalgic sound that they'll give you the all-overs and a few tears. Then Homer comes in with his natural wit and story or two like he's included in this book, and he makes you happy all over again. He is funnier than he knows he is with his northeast Tennessee speech and manner, back-home stories, wonderful timing, and the sense of comedy that he picked up from Knoxville's *Mid-Day Merry-Go-Round*, and *The Grand Ole Opry*.

Anywhere you see Homer-at Bluegrass festivals, craft fairs, concerts, on the street, or in his shop-he'll charm you with his personable ways, his sharp wit, his humorous stories. One reason we all like Homer is that he likes us-all kinds of people, like those in the stories he relates in this book. You'll find out here what tickles Homer, and it will tickle you too.

Loyal Jones
Berea, Kentucky

Acknowlegements

My heartfelt thanks to my daughter Cindy Lowy who inspired and encouraged me to write this book. She also so graciously volunteered her valuable time to paint the book cover, pencil the illustrations, and compose the poem *Time Passages.*

My special thanks also goes out to Walter Johnson without whose enthusiasm and encouragement this book would not have been a reality. He has encouraged me every step of the way. He also served as a photographer and editor-in-chief. I also wish to thank William Johnson for his photography and his masterful work digitally recording the enclosed compact disc (CD), Michael Johnathon for allowing me to use live recordings from the Woodsongs Old Time Radio Hour, and cousins Nannie Mae Ledford and Charles Ledford for photos submitted.

A special thanks to my son-in-law Dan Baker for the design of the cover; Colista Ledford, Mark Ledford, Cindy Lowy, Julia Baker, and Mattie Lee Conkwright for letting me use their poetry; and Jerry Schureman for photography.

I deeply appreciate Loyal Jones, Ron Pen, Michael Johnathon, Loretta Sawyer, and Judge Ray Corns for their endorsements. Lastly, but not least, I wish to thank my loving wife Colista for her support and encouragement all along the way. She has always been my best supporter and given me more strength, and perseverance than I could have ever had on my own.

Introduction

I have loved the idea of story telling for a long time. It goes back to when my Uncle Otis, who lived just down over the hill, would come up to our house and have me go out on our porch and tell me numerous stories of things that happened to him growing up. As I listened to those stories, they made an indelible impression on my mind. That impression and the fact that my daughter, Cindy, wrote a book, led me to thinking I might also try my hand at writing.

The first thing I did was write down one of Uncle Otis' stories using a modern new-fangled machine called a computer. I showed that story to some friends who seemed to know a lot about writing, and they said right away that I ought to put some of those stories into book form. The more I thought about it, the more I thought I might do so. With the passing of time, I began to remember a lot of things that had happened to me as well as the stories Uncle Otis relayed to me and began to write them down. Some of the stories are very dear to me. Some are funny, some are a little sad, but they represent memories of my growing up and history of the area in those days.

I have made no attempt to "polish-up" these tales grammatically — just put them down as I remember them. I sincerely hope you get as much enjoyment out of reading them as I did writing them.

This book has turned out to be a family project since I have included poetry written by my wife and children.

I have included a compact disc of some of my favorite music.

Further Up the Creek

By Mark L. Ledford

Come join me, dear friend, for a walk through the glade,
Down to the creek bed where once we all played.
We'll start at the spring just over the ridge,
And make our way past the old swinging bridge.

Take care where you step, for the path's not as clear
As it was years ago when we first ventured here.
Be still — can you hear it? Just take a good look.
Those babbling sounds...we're nearing the brook!

Though decades have passed, my memory's still good
Of the long summer days we spent in this wood —
Sitting on the bank just dreaming and wishing.
Abandoning chores for some leisurely fishing.

Hunting and catching small crawdads and frogs,
Climbing and leaping off old fallen logs.
Searching for stones that were just right for skipping,
Shedding our clothes — to go skinny dipping!

Rafting on inner tubes down to the bend,
Playing cowboys and Injuns until the day's end.
Those days filled our lives with such complete pleasure,
And gave us these memories that we will long treasure.

Well, time travels on, and so must I,
But before we part and say 'goodbye,'
I pray that you'll reach all the goals that you seek,
Until we meet again — further up the creek.

A Day in the Life of Homer C. Ledford — That's me.

Sometimes it just doesn't pay to get up in the morning! "If it wasn't for bad luck, I'd have no luck at all!"

I was just a "young sprout" when this all took place, only about fourteen-years-old at the time. It seemed that I was Dad's favorite "go do this, go do that" person. My older brother, Paul, and I were the only ones left at home to help Dad with the chores. Although he was willing, Dad was just too short and "dumpy" to do much. He was a little on the heavy side for his height, you know, and Paul would use every excuse to trap me into doing the hard chores.

Well, this particular morning it all began to happen. I was sleeping so peacefully and dreaming of all the nice things a teen-ager could dream about — fishing, playing my guitar, oh yeah, pretty girls too! All that good stuff came to a screeching halt when I heard Dad's voice. Now this was not his prize winning hog calling voice, but it didn't miss it by much.

"Homer, git outta' that bed and lets greet the morning, boy!"

"Oh, Dad let me sleep just a little while longer. I'll get up soon."

He didn't say another word — just left. Knowing Dad like I did, that put a little worry in my noggin. The next thing I knew here came Dad with a big long peach tree limb, and introduced me to it. He warped me across the legs a couple of good whacks and boy, did that smart. I wasted no

time in springing out of that
soft bed, grabbing my overalls.
It didn't matter that I got them
on backwards, I just needed to
get to that breakfast table fast.

So I ate a pretty good breakfast and was feeling better by
now. But wait. Dad says, "Boys,
we gotta' get that wash water
carried up from the spring for
your mother to do her washing
today." That was bad news because that spring was straight
over the hill about a quarter of
a mile and we had to carry
about fifty gallons of that clear
sparkling spring water up that
hill requiring about five trips. I
think that took a good hour at

*I recently returned to the spot
across the road from our house
where we hauled water from the
spring.*

the pace we went, but it seemed like it took three times that
long.

I felt pretty spent after all that and felt like maybe I would
get a break and play the radio a few minutes. Some mighty
fine country music was usually playing on that favorite
Nashville station. Huh-uh, didn't work like that.

"Homer, go harness up ole Tobe (Tobe was our long-
legged mule which I didn't trust.) and lets get ready to plow
the corn. I think it's going to rain this afternoon and we have
to have that done right away." Oh, well, here we go again.

After struggling through about four miles of corn, it was
time for "dinner" (lunch), so I yelled at Paul who was plowing in the field next to mine, "Lets go Paul, it's chow time."
Paul climbed on old Kit, our other mule, and with me on ole
Tobe, we headed to the spring over the hill to water the mules.
I didn't notice the big cedar tree just over the hill and doggone it, ole Tobe went right under that tree and the big limbs
drug me off. I hit hard. I landed kinda' angling on my left
jaw and felt like I had broken it. I got up crying. And you

know what? Paul started laughing at me and to tell you the truth I almost felt like relieving him of the responsibility of living! That thought only lasted a moment though, and finally we arrived at the house and ate a good meal.

After dinner, I got permission to go the post office which was a mile away, to see whether my guitar had come that I had ordered from a mail order catalog. No, it hadn't but you know on the way back I took to running so I wouldn't be late to go to the field and boy that was a mistake! I stubbed my bare foot on a big rock sticking up out of that old wagon road and made a big "stone bruise" on my foot. Man, now that was trouble! But you know what? Dad let me off the rest of the day! Dad had a good heart after all.

After supper Paul wanted me to play checkers with him but I just simply didn't have the strength left. All I wanted to do was go to bed and I did. I just hoped the new day coming would be better than the one that just ended.

We'll see, right?

The Ledford clan gathered for a photograph at our fiftieth wedding anniversary celebration in 2002. From left are our daughters, Mattie Lee Conkwright and Cindy Lowy, Colista, me, our daughter, Julia Ann Baker, and our son, Mark.

In this photograph taken on our front porch in 1954 by The Nashville Tennessean, I'm playing one of my dulcimers for my mother, Ova Ledford, and my wife, Colista.

My parents, Abe and Ova Ledford, on their wedding day, September 21, 1913.

A Lady

Everyone knows someone they can say good things about and I can tell you about such a person. She lived in the foothills of the Upper Cumberlands, part of the Appalachian chain. She never had much, pretty much lived in poverty but in those days you didn't call it that. Her husband owned a small "truck farm" but really didn't know how to farm. He could plow, harrow, raise some corn and cane for sorghum molasses, but that was about it.

This lady always did the washing for the four kids on an old hand scrubbing wash board. She walked to the store to get the few groceries such as coffee, salt, and sugar, or whatever was needed. The walk took her down a very rugged steep hill, across the swinging bridge over the river, and up the steep hill for about a half a mile to the gravel "highway." It was two more miles to the store on the gravel road.

When any of the kids were sick, she would do whatever needed to be done for them, bathe their foreheads, bandage up cuts on their feet from going barefoot in the summer, make her own medicines such as mixing molasses, vinegar and herbs for coughs, colds or whatever.

This lady I knew never complained about her husband dumping the dirt from his old shoes on the living room floor, throwing his overalls in the corner for her to pick up and hang across the wash tub, and she always was right there in the kitchen cooking the meals on time — if there was anything to cook. Lots of times it was left over pinto beans and corn bread and a little milk.

Sometimes she would not feel so well herself, but never let it get her down. She went right on doing her chores as usual unless she was bedfast.

This "saint" was a very religious person. She and her husband always took the children to church every Sunday and sometimes when there was a revival, they went every night of the week. What a great bearing this had on the children. They learned what true love and caring was all about, and to this day I think that was a true blessing.

She was such a loving and caring person herself. She took care of her mother after her brother moved out and no longer cared for her. Folks around said she was one of the finest people, along with her husband, there was around. She knew almost everybody and was friends with most anybody that would be friendly.

I know this all to be true about this lady — because she was my mother!

Mother, Ova Ledford, playing the autoharp about 1920.

Mother's Flowers

Sometimes relationships are one hundred percent perfect, and sometimes they are not. That was the way it was with Mom and Dad. The latter leaned toward being set in his ways, if not a little stubborn. Mother was very sweet natured and most everything suited her just fine most of the time. There were times, however, when she got fussy with Dad. She would throw in just a little bit of nagging here and there too, and of course, Dad would take exceptions to that.

Mother had a lot of love in her and showered it upon Dad, but she loved her flowers almost to a fault. She had a bad habit, according to Dad, of planting her flowers right down the middle of the garden, right to the fence on both ends. The garden was laid out in one big square about three hundred feet both ways. The only problem was it made it difficult, if not impossible, for dad to plow the garden in the spring without plowing up some of mother's prized flowers. The mules would take up about eight feet of space, the plow another five, then there was dad added on, requiring about fifteen feet to turn at the ends.

This one time I remember, I guess I was thirteen- or four-teen-years-old when spring had rolled around, and it was time to plow the garden. Gosh Dad dreaded that chore! He harnessed up the ole mules, Tobe and Dinah. I called Dinah "Dynamite" because she was "heady and fast." Dad hitched them to the "turning plow" in readiness for the big job. The plow had two handles that curved down at the ends to make it easier to hold on to and guide it. There was a "tongue," a slightly curved steel beam that served as a "keel-like fixture that the curved or twisted steel slats were attached to at the bottom. These all came to a point, which in use, would make the plow go into the soil and turn it over.

With a nervous yell, "Get up Tobe, Dinah," Dad entered and tackled that garden head on.

He plowed the first row and everything was fine, but wait! On the second round the mules had to turn too short and up came some of mother's flowers. It just so happened that mother was watching from the kitchen window and saw the destruction. Wow!! The "fat was in the fire" then! She almost burst through that old flimsy screen door, across that rough planked back porch and out to the garden fence right up close to my very nervous and frustrated Dad. Mother screamed, "Abe Ledford, you've done it again! Plowed up some of my prettiest flowers! Can't you ever learn? Dad, who had already tightened up, was frustrated and a little short on temper, yelled back, "Old woman, if you can do it any better, here are the mules and here is the plow!" With that, mother ducked back into the house and didn't dare to show herself again!

You know what? Dad politely took those mules and plow and went straight to the barn. No more said, except after a while we heard him praying aloud to the top of his voice in the hallway of the barn. I don't think he was praying to us either, just from what he was saying.

What it was, as he had been known to do in the past when he thought he had done something wrong, was praying for forgiveness. Dad really was a good Christian man and always tried to do the right thing.

Well, before the day was over, the garden got plowed, and most of the flowers were still standing. Mother simmered down, and the sun settled down very beautifully in the west, and all was peaceful again.

The Little Brown Shack

The little wagon road ran from the main gravel road down to the creek, up the hill past Uncle Tom's house on the left, up past Mr. Smith's, and winding through the graveyard, went down past Uncle Bugg's house. Taking a right turn about three hundred yards further, and through some sassafras bushes and up to our house on the hill. To the left was the old weather-beaten barn and corn crib, and just to the right of the house was the "smoke house" where the meat was kept.

Well, I want you to know, directly behind the house was the little shack we called the "place of rest," the "privy." Some today might call it an out-house or toilet!

This little building I built myself and I thought I would really do the job right, and make it as usable as possible. Yes, that's right, I made it a "two-holer." I'm not saying that two people would use it at the same time though, but it was available in case of emergencies.

Speaking of emergencies, my mother just so happened to see the need to use this little house one stormy summer day. With the little door closed and everything in order, she went ahead and minded her own business. Well, sometimes those little storm clouds came rather sudden in that country since you really couldn't see them because of the trees surrounding the house. This was one of those times. Before Mother knew it, a storm cloud was up and raging before she got everything settled with nature. Oh, yes, it started to lightning and thundering and striking everywhere it seemed. The first thing Mother knew it had struck a tree right close to where she was sitting. Yep, you never heard such a blast! Mother jumped up and declared the whole building had exploded! Everybody ran to see what was the matter, don't you know. Mother was as white as a bunch of sheets and couldn't tell us much for some time. Finally getting her senses back together and with a slightly clear mind, she told us what had happened as near as she could.

I'm telling you we like to have never gotten Mother to trust that "two holer" again. She thought the barn was safer, and the rest of us kinda agreed with her!

A family group picture taken during our reunion in 2002 in Tennessee.

The Book

By Homer C. Ledford
It always laid on the table
Right beside mother's bed.
It never had to be dusted —
This book.

No clutter around it
Evidence of careful
Handling,
But used!

This book contained much —
Births, deaths,
Marriages, events,
And all written by hand.

Yes, it told how to live a good life,
How to treat your fellow man.
There were passages of history
Ancient or present.

Yes, it told of Jesus'
Birth and death,
The resurrection.
You could read
About the beginning of man,
And of good and evil.

Yes, this great book was —
Mother's old Family Bible!

The swinging bridge over the West Fork River.

The Old Swinging Bridge

Our house sat right on top of the river hill. The old barn and corn crib were next, just before you headed down the hill. About ten feet beyond the barn was a barbed wire fence and then our farm went nearly straight down over the hill. You had to negotiate several little "jut outs" of stone, one log that had fallen across the path due to the ice storm the past winter, across a little creek, and there you were at the West Fork of the Obey River.

Now there were three or four different ways to cross that river. You could wade it where it was about waist deep, ride a mule, take a wagon, or yes, you guessed it, use the bridge.

This bridge I am about to tell you about was not just your common everyday bridge. It had huge one-inch diameter cables stretched in parallel from one big bluff of rock to the other. It was so solid it was just like God holding on with both hands. The floor of the bridge was supported by means of cables, or wires that were attached to the cables and down to wooden cross members onto which the flooring was nailed. Now I tell you it was solid! The only thing, you wouldn't want to get several people on it, all jumping up and down at the same time because it would throw you right out in the river if it didn't come unattached from the moorings at the end!

Some people were afraid to cross the bridge due to their fear of high places or just plain thought it might fall with them since it would sway a little. Mother was one of those. She wouldn't allow anyone else on the bridge while she was on it. If they got on it with her, she would let out a scream which could be heard all the way up to my uncle's store a mile away.

Sometimes the river would "get up" and boy it was exciting to say the least. It was interesting to see what that swollen river would bring down with it. We, meaning us kids, would get in the middle of the bridge and watch the show. Here came chicken coops, oil barrels, "out houses," (I'm not kidding!) chickens, and I just don't know what all else! It was one of these big floods that took out the original bridge because it was swung too low. Once a large tree was washed down and almost got the new bridge. It did brush the lower side of it a little.

After many years, the bridge finally got a name. It was called the "A.H. Copeland Bridge" because my uncle, Abe Copeland, who owned the local store gave the money to construct it. He was the only one around there that had the funds to do so. Uncle Abe married my dad's only sister, Aunt Nannie.

Today that bridge is no longer in use. It became unsafe due to deterioration of the planking and rusting of the main supporting cables. And too, other roads have been built and there is no longer a need to cross the river at that location.

One thing for sure, I will never forget swinging with that old bridge and all the memories that goes with it.

Cindy Lowry 04

The Bell

There are so many things in a community that stand out big and make a dent in one's consciousness so to speak. These are things like people, natural carvings called hills and mountains, the winding streams that snake along through those hills, old buildings such as churches with their steeples so high they seem to punch through the fleecy white clouds, and old houses covered with well worn wooden shingles that are home to some of the old folks we know. And there was the old church/school BELL!

Let me tell you about this special bell. It hung way up in the bell tower in our old school house that also served as our church. It had a big crank shaped "handle" attached to it and from that hung a long rope that reached all the way down in the room so you could pull it and make that thing ring! Just to take a look at that bell would make your eyes "bug out like a tromped on toad." It was some big bell! It measured about four feet across the bottom and approximately five feet high. Just guessing, I'll bet it weighed 1,500 to 2,000 pounds! To me the clapper looked more like a small bowling ball hanging from a metal pot holder hook, you know, the kind they used to hang the old bean pot on for cooking beans in the fireplace.

When you put that bell to ringing, I declare it was some sound. You could hear it for miles around if the wind was right. Maybe it was my imagination, but I honestly believe that bell rang in the key of C!

"Old Clapper" sure meant a lot to the Ivyton, Tennessee community where I lived and served it well. The school house was also used for church gatherings. The bell was rung when it was time for school, time for church, funerals and emergencies.

I'll never forget when the school house caught on fire. There were a bunch of us kids and we were scared to death. What happened was the old pot bellied wood burning heating stove overheated causing the smoke pipe that ran through the roof to overheat and catch the old wood shingles on fire.

The teacher saved the day by ringing the old bell. Three rings was the proper signal for emergencies. About everybody in the neighborhood came running and with the help of us kids carrying water from the nearby spring, we put out the fire! What an exciting day it was. The teacher closed the school for the day and told us kids we could "hoof" it on home, which we gladly did!

Yes, "Old Clapper" is still ringing in my mind today, and I don't care a bit because I also like the key of "C!"

Hollerin' or Using the Telephone

Communication — yes, that's what some people called it, but us folks in the mountains just called it "getting in touch," "visitin'," or just "hollerin'" to let off steam! Whatever, it worked for us.

Folks in the mountains loved to get together and visit, spread gossip about anybody and everybody they could think of, talk of church, kids, someone's love life, or whatever.

When we were out of salt, coffee, kerosene to burn in our lamps, chewing tobacco, or any of the essentials like that, we would just "holler" across the pasture to my Uncle Bugg's house, across the creek up toward the mountain to Sally Cooper's, or down the other way toward the river to Grandma's house.

Now the hollerin' I'm talking about was not the toned down version you would use to call up ole Rover. No sir. The volume was turned up to a deafening squeal. You could hear it plumb out of the county, I'm here to tell you. I can just hear it now when Aunt Virgie, Uncle Bugg's wife, would holler over to our house when she needed lamp oil.

"Abe Ledford, ABE LEDFORD, you got any lamp oil fer tonight, I'm plumb out?"

Mother would be the one to answer back. She could scream the loudest. She'd yell back, "Is that you Virgieeee?"

Well, it would go on like that until everything was understood and worked out.

People 'round there didn't live very close together. Most everybody lived at least a mile apart, and it was kinda' difficult to get the word out. There was a definite need for a better way.

One day, as if by a miracle, it happened. Word got out around there that they were going to build a telephone line to everybody's house who wanted it. Telephone was a strange foreign word to most of us, and we didn't see how anything like that could happen.

Well, sure enough, along came a couple of fellers, all dressed up like going to a funeral or something, and talked to my dad and described all the things that were going to happen. Dad took all this with a grain of salt and just put himself in "park." Like the others around there, seeing was believing and Dad hadn't seen anything yet.

But you know, the first thing we knew, here came an old Model T Ford truck all loaded down with rolls of wire, poles, brackets, nails and I don't know what all, and dumped them down right in our front yard. Now things were getting exciting!

The holes were drilled, posts set up, wire strung from one pole to another until there it was — we were connected. Those wires were stretched so tight you could almost play a tune on them!

After the wires were all up, now came the hookup. In order to do that there had to be something to hook onto. Well, sure enough they brought in this funny looking box with a "horn" in the front of it and a crank on the side. It was a pretty thing, all polished up and made of the finest "quartered" oak they said. I wanted right away to start winding it up so it would talk , but they told us we couldn't because there was no spring to wind up. They said with a few lessons, we would know how to operate it. I had my doubts.

The "technicians" had us sit down around the table there and began to lay out the instructions. It proved to be fairly simple. Of course, anything is simple when you know how!

The first thing you did, we found out, was to figure out a signal to use when someone else wanted to call us. It was all based on how many cranks you did. You would crank three times for our connection, four for someone else's, and so on. Oh yes, there was an emergency ring consisting of six real short rings. There was one real long ring for a party line. This was easy to remember. Too easy, I might add, because there was a tendency for some around there to listen in on your conversation. One lady up on the hill from us just loved to hear what was going on. She was minding everyone else's business and her's too!

So it was, there was very little reason for anyone to yell or holler anymore because now we had gone "high tech." We kinda' missed the personal contact though!

Uncle Bugg's house, at left, was over the hill and across the pasture from the our house, above right, but was still within hollerin' range.

Cindy, Colista and I pose for a photograph in front of the our old homeplace while a current resident looks on.

Granny Gets a "Crank" Call!
(Fictitious)

Back in the early days in the mountains, there was occasionally some new development such as a battery powered radio, spring wound phonograph, and, yes, the "party line," hand cranked, battery operated telephone. Now these telephones were something else. It was a big box-like contraption fastened to the wall sporting a horn-like affair to talk into, and a stretched out funnel shaped gadget that you could put to your ear and listen. Oh yes, and it had a crank on the side to do the ringing with. It was great for getting the word back and forth but with some disadvantages, namely one being everybody could listen in and/or gossip.

Here is one likely conversation that would take place between two parties.

Riiiiiiiiiing——Riiiiiiiiiiiiiiiing——Ring—Ring!

"What in tarnation! Here I am with my hands in the biscuit dough down here in the kitchen and the blasted phone rings. Who in the world could be calling at this hour, and what fer? I never know'd it to fail, when I'm the busiest that new fangle contraption rings off the wall."

"Hello, Hello, uh, huh. Whadja say? Who is this? Well, I'll be doggoned, Sari, Is that you? You know Sari, I just got started making me some biscuit pone for the old man's breakfast and I
jist don't have time fer any of yore gossipin'."

"Well, let me tell you. This is one time you'd better listen and listen but good! Do you know that old man up the holler that makes 'moonshine'? Well, I seed him going 'round with that widder woman down the creek, and I tell you the 'sparks' were somewhat flying! Why the other day, I was out gatherin' some kindling wood for my stove, and don't you know I seed them holdin' hands, of all things, right out in plain daylight, don't you know! Now, Grants (nickname for Granny), ain't that a scandal you ain't heard about?"

"Sari, I shore hain't. You're the first one to tell me. I wish I may never! Holding hands, eh? What's this world comin' to this day and time. A decent feller can't put a foot outside without being embarrassed to pieces. My Ma and Pa woulda' kilt me if they caught me holding hands with a feller — anyplace! I did, but they never caught me.

Sari, soon's I get my old man's breakfast and all, I will be right up there, and we can discuss these outrageous goings on. Don't you tell anybody else about this 'til I get there, you hear?"

"Gosh Grants, I shore won't. Oh, by the way, I got a couple more wayward souls to report on too. So git yore ears cleaned out real good and ....!

Granny McDonald breaking beans on her front porch. Photo was taken when I was a boy.

Our First Radio

There wasn't much "high tech" equipment to be found in the little community of Ivyton, Tennessee. If you were looking for it, it just couldn't be found except for the dinner bell that set up on top of the post with the rope hanging down to pull when mother wanted to "ringy, ringy" us from the field or whatever we were doing, to come and eat. I'm not going on record to call that real "high tech" though. However, it beat hollering your lungs out.

It wasn't long though before we were introduced to some "high tech" equipment in the form of battery powered radios. Oh, but that was something. It created a stir and a whole lot of excitement. My cousin, Houston Ledford, was the first to be able to own one. He saved up his money from truck driving and bought one of the prettiest ones that I had ever seen.

It had a little dial right in the middle of the cabinet, complete with a pointer and light making it easy to select the stations, I reckon. There were two buttons, or knobs as they called them, down near the bottom. I think they said they were selection knobs. I learned later that they were used to change the volume and to select the stations. The cabinet was of real pretty wood, at least to my notion, and it was rounded off at the top, kinda' egg shaped. Houston and Uncle Tom would invite kinfolks and neighbors to come around and listen to the Grand Ole Opry on Saturday nights. We went also. That sure was some fine music. We wanted one real bad!

Finally, it came to pass that we managed to save up a little money from selling hen eggs and digging may apple root that we sold to my Uncle Abe Copeland's store to buy us a new fangled radio, that is if we didn't want to get too fancy. Well, we had a mail order catalog that we sometimes would order from because items were so cheap, and, lo and behold, there was a real pretty radio they had on sale, and our money was just enough to cover the cost, shipping and all.

I visited the post office everyday looking for our treasure and finally it came. It took about four days for it to get there as I remember. The total cost was $18. Yes, that included the battery.

We wasted no time plugging in that battery and turning it on. This was in the summer and in those days there was no FM, so there was a lot of static. It was hard to hear anything real clear, but we were willing to put up with the static anyway. We picked up all kinds of stuff — the news, weather, and music, mostly from Nashville. We got to messing around with the middle button, and what do you know, that was the knob to bring in short wave stations. First thing we heard was a station in Quito, Ecuador. That was something. We couldn't understand a thing they said, but honestly we enjoyed the music!

It was bound to happen. Grandma found out about our new "high tech" outfit and thought she would come up and listen. She didn't believe that you could hear someone like that and them so far away.

Grandma arrived on Saturday night, and we were sitting around the machine ready to go. Grandma pulled her chair up close and said, "Now prove what you been tellin' me."

The switch was flipped and on came H.V. Kaltenborn with the news. It was 6 p.m, and that was always his time to give the news.

Grandma said, "Turn that thing around so's I can see him."

"Grandma, you can't see him. He's in Washington."

Now you see, Grandma knew something about where Washington was.

"Lordy, Honey, they hain't no way that man can be in Washington. Why he's got to be right here in that box. Let me talk to him. Mr. Kaltenborn, is that you in there?"

"Grandma, I told you, he's not actually here. It's all done by electricity traveling through the air — sound waves, just like you might see ripples on the water."

"Is 'at so. I still don't git it, but if you say so. I know one thang, I hain't gonna' git me none of them thar thangs. I'm afraid of 'em. Why, if that thang ketched on fire, it could burn yore house down. They hain't no tellin' what might happen to a feller!"

We later turned on the Grand Ole Opry, a very popular show out of Nashville, Tennessee, so she could listen to the music. She pulled that old rocker up real close, propped her right foot up on the little stool sitting there, and sucked in the music of the Fruit Jar Drinkers and The Gully Jumpers, two old-time string bands that performed on the Grand Ole Opry. And she got to hear the Solemn Ole Judge do his announcing. What a time! What a treat!

But I'll never forget Grandma's reactions when that new fangled, "high tech" machine was turned on! I don't think she ever understood what was going on inside that radio, but she listened anyway!

My First Christmas

I have many good memories of growing up in the mountains, called the Southern Appalachian region of Tennessee. Why, we lived so far back in the hills they had to "pipe daylight in to us!" Why, I remember Dad getting lost just going to the barn to feed the stock. One time it came a snow storm and the wind blew the snow so hard that we couldn't see Dad coming from the barn. We had to ring the old cowbell to make sure he found us.

I guess one of the best recollections I have is when I experienced my first Christmas at school. I was in the first grade (or as they called it then, the primer), and Christmas time rolled around. Our teacher, who was slightly related to us, told the class we just had to have a Christmas tree. There were more boys than girls in school so she elected us four cousins, Ray McDonald, Charles and Kenneth Ledford, and me to go fetch a nice cedar tree.

We set out with our little hatchet in hand, some rope and a whole lot of determination. We walk about two miles along the creek to find the prettiest tree that ever grew. We really wouldn't have had to go all that far but we kinda liked being out of school, you know.

We finally came upon a nice grove of some of the prettiest cedar trees you ever laid your peepers on. I was pretty handy with a hatchet so I was elected to chop down the prize. This tree was about eight feet high and quite unhandy about moving so guess what, Ray, the biggest and bossiest one of the bunch, said we would have to hook up like a team of mules and drag the tree to the school house. Ray said, "You all pull and I will drive, just to make things work out." We didn't argue with him since he was the one with the whip.

A couple of hours later, we arrived back at school and when the teacher saw the tree where it had been dragged along on it's side in the mud, she almost had a "conniption fit" backwards! We blamed Ray since it was his idea all along.

The teacher gathered up her smarts and figured she would just turn the bad side of the tree to the wall, and of course that worked very smoothly. We tied the top of the tree to the ceiling and nailed the trunk to the floor (just a rough plank floor, mind you), making the whole thing fairly secure.

We decorated this fine piece of art with cotton, some old left-over roping from another year, put on a few small candles, and even lit them, if you can believe that! I don't know why we didn't burn the whole place down, but we didn't. The good Lord was with us, I guess.

Apparently, Santa Claus came that night because when we arrived at school the next morning, toys and pretty gifts were piled all around the tree. My, my! What a sight that was for us!

Finally it came time for the gifts to be passed out. I was so excited, I became as nervous and jumpy as a rabbit's nose. My name finally was called and there it was, a nice big wooden duck on wheels, all painted so realistic, and it even quacked when pulled along. Boy, what a Christmas!

A few years have passed now, but I still look forward to Christmas because I love to see the faces of my grandchildren as they gather around the tree to open their gifts.

Sari Phortune

It wasn't hard to get there from my house. You just walked across our pasture field, past Uncle Bugg's house, across the little creek and up the hill about one quarter mile and there you were. You could tell when you were at the right place because all of a sudden the ground leveled off and there was a giant coffee tree in the front yard. The house looked like it was built in the nineteenth century and may have been from the looks of the big yellow poplar logs used in the structure. It had a large front porch and a small abbreviated back porch.

You'd go inside and there was Mrs. Sari Phortune, the fortune teller. Most people called her "Ole Sari." However, I don't believe they meant for that name to have the highest respect for her, but Ole Sari was a pretty decent person. She believed in the Bible and always had one lying on the table right beside her corn shuck bed. In those days most of the folks around there, including our family, didn't have store bought mattresses, they just crammed corn husks (shucks) into bed ticking and made their own. She could quote a lot of scripture, but sometimes when she got real mad, she would quote some that didn't exactly fit Bible text.

I guess Sari's most outstanding accomplishment, according to the folks around there, was she could tell fortunes by reading palms, interpreting coffee grounds that had been poured out on the saucer, and reading tea leaves.

Boy, she was real good at reading palms. I remember on one occasion I let her take a stab at reading my palm. I was only ten- or twelve-years-old at the time. She pointed out that according to the lines in my right hand that I would marry some day and have four kids. She was right on the money! Now that could've been a shot in the dark, but we'll never know, will we?

I think Sari might have had some help in getting the facts on folks when she was telling their fortunes. I say this is because she really loved to listen in on other folks conversations on the old crank type telephone party line.

Sari didn't have a lot to do most of the time so she would tune right in on what was going on in the neighborhood! I remember my grandma was on the phone one time and I heard her yell, "Sari, would you hang that dang thing up? I know you're listening!" Grandma would hear the click and that was that!

Some thought Sari Phortune was a witch. I guess it was her wearing a black dress most of the time, having a frail looking body frame, long nose that kinda crooked downward that reminded one of a hawk bill, and her black hat that looked more like a funnel with a brim on it than a hat! Also, her voice crackled so much it sounded a whole lot like static on a battery powered radio. I guess when I think about it, one could allow as how she could have been a witch! Other than all that, Ole Sari was a right good gal!

Tales of Misadventures with My Cousins

My cousins, Charles, Ken, John and I, the rotten eggs, had lots of fun together. We lived about one mile apart so it was easy for us to get together. And we did most every Sunday afternoon. However, lots of times Charles and I would show up for lunch at Uncle Bill's house and play or get into some kind of trouble the rest of the afternoon.

We especially liked to eat dinner there because Aunt Ruby was one of the best cooks in the country and had lots of good food to cook. I could count on a heaping plate full of fried potatoes, corn on the cob, chicken and dumplings, green beans, and a big slice of lemon meringue pie or chocolate pie! Boy, it's making me hungry right now just thinking about it!

My cousins (from top left) Charles, John and Kenneth sat still long enough in 1938 for photographs.

Another reason we liked to go to Uncle Bill's house was because there was so much for us to play with and get into. There was the creek just over the hill, the old buggy, caves, a barn full of hay bales, hay stacks in the nearby field, corn cobs, rotten eggs in the chicken house (Aunt Ruby always left at least one egg in the hen's nest to make the hens go back in there and lay their eggs where she wanted them to.) and on and on, far into the night! Wow! What a life!

One time the four of us were playing cops and robbers and Ken was the cop. Ken always had to be the cop. I reckon it was because it was at his house. Charles, John, and I had broken, or at least bent the law, according to Ken, so he was rounding us up and was successful in catching me. He sneaked up on me. But, Charles took off like a scared "haint" and had just gotten to the corner of the chicken house when Ken pulled a rotten egg from his coat pocket and let Charles have it. That thing exploded like an atomic bomb! I'll have you know that thing splashed all over Charles and to make things worse, he was wearing a brand new leather jacket. To say that Charles was upset is putting it mildly. He started crying, said a few choice words, most of which we didn't understand, but he didn't cuss. One statement we did understand, "I'm going home!" And he did!

Boy, things got "rotten in the State of Denmark" then! Soon as Uncle Bill found out about it, he yelled at Ken (even included me) a lot in his high pitched voice, and told us we couldn't play anymore and introduced us to Ken's room for the next three hours. Boy that really hurt! I really don't know what happened to Charles and his new coat after that. I could only imagine Aunt Verlie had a large economy sized "tizzy fit," which she could do if she got "riled" real good!

Cob Fighting

I don't think cob fighting was listed as a true sport in the record books, but cob fighting was practiced in the hills of Tennessee where I grew up anyway. You had to have lots of cobs around to fight with and Uncle Bill's place was a prime battleground. Gosh, he had corn cobs scattered everywhere, in the barn lot, around the chicken house and even where he fed some of his cattle that ran loose. Well, I was going to say there was another place, but I'll skip that one. Now the hog lot was a special place for us to play. It was nice and level, had lots of good soggy cobs and of course, four or five hogs to aggravate.

As I have told you before, there was Ken, his brother John,

Cousin Charles and me. We were always getting into trouble it seems. On this particular Sunday afternoon right after eating a great meal like only Aunt Ruby could cook up, the four of us couldn't find enough to occupy our time so trouble here we came! We decided to go out to the old hog lot and roust up a good game of cob fighting. I don't know if you could call cob fighting a game, it was more like a young war.

It took us a minute to decide who was going to fight who. We decided to see who could throw a good ole wet soggy cob the farthest. Charles and I lost so we sided up against Ken and John. We lined up facing each other about thirty-five feet apart, just a good throwing distance mind you, and the war began. Boy did we have plenty of ammunition. Those cobs were plenty wet and soggy too! There were no rules so we just started throwing those nasty cobs at each other right off the bat. Now these cobs were not of the "nubbin" sized caliber. They were big ones. Uncle Bill fed the hogs the biggest ears of corn he could find. He wanted to fatten them boogers up real good for the winter you know!

The cobs were whizzing by me most of the time. None of us were really that good a shot. A quick thought came across my mind. I thought I'll just show Ken what a good aim I am, so I stooped down and started to pick up a special block buster to let him have it. Just as I raised up to launch mine, ole Ken let me have it right between the eyes with a "Ledford Special," as he called it. Now that smarted enough so that I began to whimper, some would call it crying, and took off toward the house.

Cob fighting was definitely against Uncle Bill's rules. He found out about it right away and came running out before we could scatter, and started "tongue lashing" us something terrible.

"Daggonnit, I can't let you out of my sight a minute but what you are into some kind of trouble. Now let me tell you this and listen good, you git in this house right now and I don't mean maybe!"

So that was that. I forgot all about whimpering. Our main problem now was when we'd ever get out of Uncle Bill's jail?

Hay Stacks

U ncle Bill had a large farm and a big portion of it was reserved for growing his hay that he fed to his stock — cattle, mules, and other animals. There was more than half of his fields were devoted to corn, also a very important grain. In order to preserve his hay so that it would last through the winter, he would put it into stacks that resembled a bullet pointing to the sky. To keep the stack from falling over, a long pointed fifteen-foot pole was set in the ground, and the hay was placed around it. A very good arrangement I must say.

On this special Sunday afternoon, I think Ken, Charles, John and I had a special "mean streak" in us 'cause we decided (I want to blame Ken for this, but I can't be sure this time.) to go up to the field where the hay stacks were and do some sliding. What we did, and we oughta' been "raw hided," was climb up on those stacks and slide off. Man, now that was fun!

Uncle Bill didn't know where we were or we would have never made it to the field. No buddy!

We slipped and slid for a while, but got tired of that, so another idea materialized. Can you believe we actually tunneled through that stack? We made holes about the size of a fifty-five gallon oil drum, but a little problem developed.

Ken climbed atop of the stack and started jumping up and down with all his might and you know what? That stack gave way just over the tunnel we had made and trapped John inside. John didn't take to that too good and started yelling at the top of his voice.

"Get me out of here! Get me out of here!"

Charles and I started pulling hay for all we was worth. I don't think Ken cared a lot, or just wanted to direct the operation. Anyway, we finally got John out, but about that time everything began to fall apart. Here came Uncle Bill and this time he had a hickory switch which looked about four feet long and began to warp Ken and John and threatened Charles and me with our lives! Here we go again back to the jail house. I guess it didn't matter so much this time because the sun was hanging low over the trees that ringed uncle Bill's house. Well, it was good while it lasted!

Riding the Calf

Charles, Kenneth and John, and I were at Uncle Bill's house that Sunday and ran out of anything to entertain ourselves with, so we put our heads together and came up with a plan to have some fun. I can't positively say that Ken was the leader of this big event, but it sure leaned a lot in that direction. Ken said, "Boys, Daddy Bill has a half-grown boy calf out in the barn stable, and if we can work it just right, we ought to be able to rope that critter and ride it like "rodeo style." Of course, the rest of us agreed. It sounded like a lot of fun to us.

So Ken found a large piece of plow line rope and we headed for the barn. There he stood, one of the finest calves you ever saw, and from our viewpoint, just raring to be ridden! Now the problem was going to be roping that "monster" and tying him down so we could mount safely.

This ole boy was not in any mood to be roped and gave us a dirty look to prove it. He stood with all four legs protruding forward, ears perked up, tail almost straight out, and those eyes looked like they were afire, and I'm not kidding! Ken had an idea, "Boys, let's see if we can't fool the ole boy. We'll just put some corn in the corner and he'll take to that like a 'hawk on a chicken'!"

That calf started eating and Ken swung that rope, and sure enough it went right around that calf's neck. "Got him!" The next thing we had to do was to get him out in the lot behind the barn where Uncle Bill couldn't see us. We knew if Uncle Bill caught us that would be pretty much the end of the line for us for sure. It took all four of us to accomplish the task, but we got him out there.

Now Ken and Charles seemed to be in charge so they told me I would have to ride him first, and besides I had the longer legs and could wrap them around the calf and hold on better. I wasn't too keen on that idea, but I finally gave in just to get started.

They tied down the ole boy to a rail in the fence and here I went. I jumped right on him like a pro and about that time he lunged, pulled the rope loose from the fence and off we went. This was real "rodeo style" all right! I was holding on to that rope, legs wrapped around his belly and doing pretty well for a brief second, but then it happened. That calf took one "western swing," two leaps upward and one quick "eastern swing" and off I came. Now that smarted! I fell on my right shoulder, and felt like I plowed a six-inch furrow right down through that muddy lot!

I finally pried myself up, shook myself off, and looked to find Ken and the others. Lo and behold they had done took off. Before I could clear the lot, here came Uncle Bill and Mr. Ledbetter who was visiting there. Uncle Bill gave me a pretty good tongue lashing. He thought that was enough punishment for me, but when he caught Ken and John, it was a good old country switching. Charles got away and went home. End of the rodeo!

Uncle Bill and Mr. Ledbetter managed to get the calf back in the stable and he didn't even get a scratch!

See Ya' Further Up the Creek

There were several first cousins that I liked very much. We grew up together and had some wonderful times. We went to the same little one room school on the hill, played together in school and after school and on Sundays. My very favorite ones to play with were Charles, whose daddy was Uncle Tom Ledford, and Uncle Bill's sons, Kenneth and "Little John." We were about the same age, but Ken was the oldest, me next, then Charles and Little John.

I think we were around fifteen-years-of-age, give or take two or three years, when this adventure took place. John was called "Little John" because he was a bit small for his age.

The school house where we got our early book learning sat on a hill just above the little creek known as Cowan Branch. That little creek was really nice, clear as crystal and real friendly looking most of the time, but look out when it came a big thunderstorm with lots of rain. Then it was "gang busters." The way the rugged mountains around there were arranged, they formed a natural funnel which sent the water right to the little creek, making it big and swift. It would wash out our footlog across the creek or anything that got in its way.

It was in the afternoon, pretty close to time for school to turn out and it came one of the biggest washouts we just about ever saw. That little creek was ferocious and wasn't ready to be tamed, I want to tell you!

After school was out, Charles and I came on out together and fully intended to go on home, but something came over us. I guess we were looking for a little adventure as kids will do sometimes.

Charles and I had built us a little flat bottom boat. It was,

A placid stream of water can become a raging torrent during heavy rains. It was on this creek that my cousin, Charles, and I tried to go white water rafting in a homemade wooden boat.

oh about six feet long and three feet wide. We had it anchored up the creek at our favorite swimming hole. It was a beautiful little place up the creek where nobody could see us from the road. We could go skinny dipping and nobody would know.

Charles came up with a big idea.

"Homer, let's go up the creek and have us a good ride in that boat. It sure would be exciting riding those waves, wouldn't it?"

"Hmm, Charles, do you reckon our mom's would care?"

Charles answered, "Not if they don't know it."

Well, it was decided, yessiree. Around the opposite side of the creek from Charles' house, there was a little road that wound around to another little tributary off the main one. I thought it would be fun to go that way so I said to Charles, "I'll SEE YA' FURTHER UP THE CREEK."

"OK. Homer, I'll see you up there."

I guess it took us about thirty minutes to make the way up to our little boat. When we got there, boy, was that boat rocking and rolling!

"Charles, that looks a little risky to me, what do you think?"

"Homer, I tell you what let's do, let's just strip down and that way we won't get our clothes wet, and too, our mothers won't be wondering where we been or nothing.

So that's just what we did. We managed to climb into that little poor excuse for a boat and guess what. Things went from bad to worse and that's putting it mildly. That boat began to rocking, weaving, dipping and in general tried it's best to shake us out! We were beginning to get quite concerned about this situation and were coming to realize we may have made a giant mistake. The only thing we had to hang onto was the little sides of the boat and a small rope we had used to tie it up with.

The next thing I knew, Charles really got scared and made a leap for it. He went right off the side of that boat and nearly took me with him. I reckon he thought he could jump to the bank. Huh uh, the bank was too far away. The water was raging and deep at that point. Charles was clinging on the rope for dear life and yelling, "Pull me back in, pull me back in!"

"Charles, I can't do it. I can barely hold on myself!"

About that time Charles was pulled loose from the rope and the water headed him down stream real fast. I yelled, "Charles, try to grab a bush or something and I'LL SEE YA' FURTHER DOWN THE CREEK!"

Like a miracle, ole Charles was able to grab onto an old stump sticking up near the bank about fifty feet away. The boat and I hung up on the old log that had fallen across the creek and I also was able to get out. Scared to death, but SAFE!

We did have enough sense to put our clothes under the overhanging cliff across the creek and kept them dry. We dressed, took out down the other side of the creek to Charles' house. Aunt Verlie hadn't even missed us. She just figured we were out at the barn playing in the hay or something.

That little episode sure taught us a huge lesson. As the old saying goes: It sure broke us from sucking eggs!

A Gentle Breeze

By Colista Ledford

Music comes in many ways
And brightens up and cheers our days.
It is the laughter of a child.
It is the wind and clouds so wild.

Music is a gentle breeze
that softly moves among the trees.
It is the robin's call at dawn.
It is the church choir's joyous song.

Music is an old man's dream
as his fingers pluck the strings.
It warms my hearth, it fills my heart
And makes me sing!

I have always loved music and musical instruments. I started making instruments out of necessity and it led to a rewarding career as a luthier. Shown here are some of the instruments I have made.

The Old Buggy

Looking back to the good ole days, the horse and buggy was a favorite mode of transportation if you could afford one. We couldn't afford it so we just rode a mule or maybe took the old farm wagon. It was bedded down with straw and had a quilt covering the straw. Dad was the driver, riding up front on what's called a "spring seat." He had to sit there to guide the mules along the way.

Uncle Andy Evans, my Uncle Bill's daddy-in-law, owned a very fine "up town" old buggy and kept it parked in Uncle Bill's lean-to shed attached to the barn. The old buggy wasn't used much any more because folks were getting older and didn't seem to want to go out much.

This particular buggy didn't have the fringe on top, but it did have some mighty nice gold paint around the edges of the wooden framework. The wheels were made of the finest white oak and sported special hammered-steel tires on them. The hammering made them very tough to withstand the wear and tear of the rough terrain they had to roll over. There was a very nice seat, all padded with some type of springy animal hair material, perhaps long hair wool from sheep or goats. The seat was supported by leaf-type springs underneath, making it more comfortable while riding over all those rocks and things. There was a real nifty top that could be laid down similar to that of a convertible car or it could be brought up to protect the riders from the elements. This was a one-horse buggy so it had two "tongues" so the horse was hooked up between them, making it easy to control the horse and buggy.

Uncle Andy, who everybody called Pa, was getting along in years. I think he was ninety-two at the time. Everybody loved him because he was so smart and treated everyone, including me, with the utmost respect. Only one thing, you didn't dare "cross" him, meaning you did whatever he said or else. I never did know for sure what the "what else" meant. I was about to find out a little about it though because Ken, Charles, John and I came close to "crossing" him one Sunday.

Now Pa really treasured that old buggy, so much so that he checked on it most every day. Well, this one Sunday, the "big four," Ken, Charles, John and I, decided to take a ride in that prized buggy. KIDS WILL BE KIDS, you know! The other three concluded that they would be the first to ride and I would pull. Now pulling was fine until you went up hill and that became a drag.

I took off down a little slope, around the corner of the barn where no one could spot us and things were going real good. Ken would yell "git up, git up" and I would go a little faster. I didn't know what a little faster would do, so I headed down hill and that regular sized buggy became a large buggy and started pushing me, and we flew right down over the hill toward the creek.

Oh, boy! Ken began to yell, "Stop this thing Domer." They used to call me Domer for a nickname.

I yelled back, "Put the brake on, I can't hold it!"

"There is no brake," Ken yelled, "It's been disconnected."

I had to think fast so I just turned loose of the tongues and took off running to get out of the way. There they went! They didn't stop until they hit the creek with a big splash. I think they knocked every fish out of that little creek!

Pa still had his hearing so he must have had it tuned in because here he came, walking stick in high gear, don't you know. When he got to us he wasn't walking without that stick. He was waving it at us with a threatening motion which we understood real well. We tried to talk ourselves out of it by putting up all kinds of tales, excuses, lies. Take your pick! It just didn't seem to work, so Ken and John took a lashing, and Charles and I went home. The safe thing to do.

There was no real damage to the buggy, but you can bet your bottom dollar that was the last time we went for a forbidden buggy ride. Could you blame us?

Brother J. B.'s Preaching and Baptizing

In the mountains where I grew up, it was customary to have week-long revivals in the little community church. We would have them about every six months, or whenever they were needed. As a result of these protracted meetings, there would be several converts, maybe six or eight, which was a lot for our size settlement. After the meetings were over, then came the baptizing, or "dunkings" as some of the folks around there called them. All four of us kids were fascinated by all this, especially my brother J.B.

J.B. was a good boy. You see, Mother and Dad always took us to church and we were adequately exposed. Sometimes J.B. would talk my other brother Paul and me into having church with him. Paul was next to me and I was the youngest. J.B. would be the preacher. At the time, Paul and I just couldn't see what we could get out of it, but went along with him just to see what he would do.

One Sunday afternoon Mother and I were sitting in the old porch swing at home just enjoying the fresh mountain air and looking at those beautiful mountains off in the distance. We had been to church that morning, ate "dinner," and just wanted to relax. J.B. had talked Paul and some of the other neighbor boys to going to the river with him to swim, or just mud crawl if you couldn't swim. Mother and Dad never seemed to mind us going to the river because we kinda' grew up in it, you might say.

Mother was reading stories to me from some of my favorite books. We had been sitting there in the swing for a good hour, when all of a sudden we heard loud intent voices coming from the river. You see the river was just straight over the hill, no distance at all. Well, don't you know after a little hard listening, Mother decided we'd better slip out to the top of the hill behind the old barn and check out what was going on.

When we got to where we could understand real well, we somewhat got our ears full! From where we were perched, we could see J.B. and all the rest and J.B was coming in loud and clear. He was standing on a stump right near the river bank and preaching his heart out! As we watched, two of the boys got "converted" and J.B. got right in the deeper water about waist deep to him, and started performing "baptisms." I mean he was "socking" them under but good! The boys were quite "touched" by all this and seemed well satisfied! Three of the other boys and brother Paul didn't seem to get in the "spirit" I guess, but that was all right because in later life they were just fine.

As we grew older, J.B. really did do some preaching on a small scale and had a great influence on all of us. I will never forget J.B.'s preaching on the stump and "baptizing."

I'm sawing away on the musical saw during a concert at the Kentucky Governor's Mansion.

Clyde

Back in my earlier days when I was still at home with Mother and Dad, I must have been around thirteen or fourteen-years-old, we often had some interesting and troublesome things happen around the place. The house where I was born and reared was a good solid one, but here and there, there were little cracks and holes between the walls and floors. I am sure the carpenters tried to do a good job, but you know, not being "finished" carpenters, they were bound to leave a little flaw now and then.

Little varmints such as mice, or possibly, even a rat, would manage to get through those cracks and holes. Yes, even snakes could slither through them! Snakes were to be avoided with a "purple passion." If Mother saw one, no matter if it was a simple black snake or a copperhead, she would yell and scream, "Bring me the hoe right quick, I've got to get rid of this thing!" As I remember, we only had one black snake come in and, of course, it was put out its misery immediately.

I don't want you to get "spooked" here, but I want to tell you we did have some mice troubles. I remember, and this was in the winter time, when we would be sitting around the cozy fireplace keeping warm, and it wouldn't be long until we would spot a little feller inching its way from the kitchen area right in the doorway leading to our living room where we were. Those little "beady" eyes were kinda' cute. As a matter of fact, it wouldn't have taken us long to take a liking to that little varmint, but we still considered it an unwelcome guest. Mother would slip out and get the broom to whack it, but it was always too fast for her. There it would go, tail flying in the air, back feet hardly touching the floor—

escaping once again! This was happening far too often and it was not acceptable! He was doing this so often that we finally gave him a name, Clyde, after one we had seen in a kid's picture book.

What to do?

Mother got to thinking on it and came up with a bright idea. Aunt Virgie McDonald who lived right across the pasture from us, had a nice big yellow tomcat, which just loved mice and not as playmates, you see. So mother went over and borrowed "Tommy." He was very gentle so she had no trouble carrying him over. He was purring so loud you could hear him a mile away. I guess he knew what was coming.

Old Tom was introduced to the kitchen area, but at first he just wanted to come in and stretch out by the warm fire. Then he finally lucked up on it. He looked up just in time to see Clyde sneaking through the door as usual. SWOOOSH! There was nothing but a yellow furry ball before our eyes. Tom disappeared through that door, into the kitchen, and I don't know where else. I know one thing though, Clyde never saw fit to pay us a visit again!

Later, Aunt Virgie was telling us about what a sweet disposition Tom had. Why, she said he had come up with one of the prettiest grins you had ever seen! That's about all he did anymore, just lay there and grin. I just wonder why.

Aunt Virgie didn't like copperheads any better than Mother did.

Typical Hillbilly Conversation
(Fictitious)

My uncle Otis McDonald met up with a friend, Mr. Jim Shumate. They were sitting on the old log house porch on the side of the hill just above the "crick" that snaked its way along down to the river. I can't say that I can understand every word they said, but it went something like this.

Otis opened the conversation, "Howdy Jim, how's thangs goin' 'round yore place?"

"Uncle Otis, we's doin' purty good, but Pap is having a lot of bothers lately. Why, the other day jist 'fore supper, I seed him jist scratching the time out of his laigs. He had his britches laigs rolled up to his knees and scratchin' with both hands fer all he wuz worth. I axed 'im whut in the worl wuz the matter, and ya' know whut he said, 'Jim, I figgered out I got the seven-year-itch and whut makes it worse, I cain't get no relief no matter where or how long I scratch. Why, look at them pore excuse for laigs! I have jist tore 'em all to smithers!

Otis says, "Jim, what in the worl are ye' goin to do for 'em?' "

Jim said, "Ya' know Otis, we pored over it a lot and finally, ole Drew Ledbetter, you know how keen he is, told us to go see Sari Phortune, the fortune teller, and she would fix us up a batch of stuff to stop them little fellers from biting like that. You know I did and she did!"

"Otis, ya' won't believe what she told Pap to use. Why she said take some old leftover hog lard,

which was already salty, add some brine salt
about whut ye' could hold in yore left hand, then
git yerself some of that thar blue stone, grind it
up into pyore powder and throw that in, stir hit
up 'til hit will be mixed proper and you have it.
Smear it all over yore self, missing nary a inch,
and that will make them little varmints weeshed
they'd never bin born!"

Ole Otis was having a hard time gittin' all this Jim was
telling 'im. He knew a little bit 'bout whut blue stone wuz.
It'll purely burn you up when you put it on yer skin like
that.

"Jim, have you tried Norie's recipe yet?"

"Yes, we did, Otis, but you know whut, Pap got rid of
his itching, but now the poor feller is something bad on fire!"
Pap said, "Fellers, I think I have finally met my fate. Instead
of going to the good place, I ended up in the other one downstairs."

Uncle Otis had his mind skinning up and down the pole
on that one and decided that the rest of his life he would be
careful of using any remedies fortune teller Sari Phortune
gave out!!.

Aunt Virgie McDonald as a young woman.

Ole Tobe

By Homer C. Ledford

It's been a long while now.
Several years to be exact
since I had the pleasure
of his company.

He will never be forgotten.
He has become a permanent
fixture in my mind.
Ole Tobe was a hard worker.

Ole Tobe was what we called him
for want of a better name.
Tobe was a powerful soul,
but had long skinny legs.

He had long ears, and
very acute hearing unless
He didn't want to
hear a command I gave.

Continued

Tobe was an especially good worker.
In the field he made it easy for me.
On the hot summer days,
he stopped at the end of
every corn row, just to
make sure I was well rested up.
I appreciated that!

Tobe was finally coming to the end
of his row, so to speak.
He was getting old now
and was no longer needed.

Yes, it was sad, for you see
Tobe was my "plow mule!"
And was being replaced by
modern ways of doing things

So long, Ole Buddy!

The Fourth of July

Everyday was a special day for me, my two brothers, Paul and J.B., and two first cousins, Ken and Charles. The Fourth of July was a very special day for us, almost as exciting as Christmas. Dad wouldn't let us go if we couldn't get the corn "laid by," meaning there could be no more weeds to chop out of the corn or plowing to do. The corn would have to be at least waist high, high enough to outgrow any weeds that might try to choke it out.

With the corn laid by and all the other chores done, we would set out to Livingston, Tennessee, which was ten miles away, to celebrate the Fourth. The only way we had to get there was hitchhiking so we would walk down the hill, cross the river on a swinging bridge and hike another mile up the hill to the old gravel road where we hoped to catch a ride. We would always get a ride, but sometimes would have to walk quite a ways before that happened.

When we finally arrived in town, the excitement really arose to a very high pitch. There were preachers on the corners, a clown or two, and one police car. One policeman was all they could afford. There were people of every description, some dressed in "overalls" as we called them, and some in suits and ties. I guess the well-dressed ones were the folks that had "made it" by selling moonshine. Others were barely dressed at all! Oh, what an experience!

There were all kinds of shows and activities going on such as raffles and poker games—the illegal type—but who cared. The beauty contests interested us boys just about the most. Boy, there was some real beauties there. We would just about give them a big "ten!" Then there were the catch-the-greasy-pig contest, which was a big crowd pleaser, and the sack race, which consisted of two "quarter wits" getting into the same gunny sack together and trying to out run the other sack racers, which usually numbered four or five pairs.

There was always a musical group playing on stage right in the center of town in front of the courthouse. Some were real good and some were not. I thought about signing up to play some, but the more I thought about it, the more I thought I wasn't good enough, or too scared, or both!

Another one of the contests that attracted a lot of attention was the husband calling contest. I had a dog in that fight because my Aunt Virgie McDonald entered it. I will never forget it either. She had a sharp piercing voice, very practiced! You see she had a great opportunity to develop it hollering for my Uncle Bugg, either to come home for lunch or dinner, or when she got real angry at him and that was pretty often mind you. Aunt Virgie, who later renamed herself Virginia for some reason, would get up on the stage down there and start "winding up" to get that voice high and screechy. She would let out a yell that could be heard all across Overton County and then some, "Buggieeeeeeee, Buggieeeeeeeeee, — She called him Buggie when she was mad at him. — Beannnnnnnnnn timmmmmmmme!" Boy she won that contest every time. It got so they wouldn't let her enter the husband calling contest, only the "fat woman" contest. She wasn't a real skinny person to put it mildly!

Well, after taking in all the activities and eating a cheap hamburger and drinking a five-cent soda pop, we were worn out and ready to call it a day.

Mom and Dad didn't like the Fourth all that much. They thought it was just a waste of time, but you know what, I think it helped us to get a better set of values, understand things around us better and helped us to grow up. Maybe I'll never know for sure, but here I am anyway.

Fear of the Graveyard

To start out with, let me tell you a little about my cousin Houston. His daddy was Tom Ledford and his mamma's name was Verlie. Tom was my Daddy's brother, making him my uncle.

Houston was a hard worker. Drove a truck for a living and was real good natured. He would do anything for you, if at all possible. I wouldn't give him a top ten rating though. You know we all have a flaw somewhere. Houston's was he imbibed too much "white lightning" on weekends now and then.

Back in Houston's "spooning" (courting) days, he was dating a cute little gal up the holler from where I lived about a two-mile walk from his place. Uncle Tom owned one of the finest, speediest hosses you ever seen, sleek, fiery-eyed and always ready to go. His name was Prince. To save time and energy, Houston rode old Prince to see his girl Priscella. I want you to know,

I demonstrate how Drew Ledbetter hid behind one of the unusual tombstones to scare Houston Ledford as he was riding to visit a "cute little gal up the holler."

Prissy—that was her nickname—was might nigh a full ten according to the judgment made by the folks around there. I was just too "green" to make a judgment like that!

Drew Ledbetter was the local joker around there and he got "wind" that Houston was going to see Prissy one night.

Houston had to ride right through the middle of the old cemetery and he didn't like that one bit because he was afraid of graveyards something terrible. "Uncle Drew," that's what they called him in those parts, would walk for miles to play a prank on somebody and that's exactly what he did to Houston.

That night about dark thirty, Uncle Drew, all decked out in a big white sheet, placed himself behind one of those high tombstones, and waited for Houston to ride by.

It wasn't long 'til here came Houston clippity-clop, clippity-clop kinda "slow on the pace." He rode up close to where Uncle Drew was and just at the right moment, Drew jumped out from behind that tombstone and let out a scream that you could hear a mile away if you were listening. I tell you it would be an understatement to say Houston was scared out of his wits! He kicked old Prince in the ribs, slapped him with the bridle strap and yelled, "Let's get outta' here Prince!"

Prince took off like a "scared haint" and was out of sight so quick it would make your head swim. They were traveling so fast that the wind friction actually lit up the darkness, according to Uncle Drew!

Uncle Tom said when Houston came home that night, he was all out of breath and white as snow in January. It took Houston a whole year to ever get to where he could tell us the whole story of what happened. One thing sure, he didn't get much more courting in with Prissy after that. He didn't marry her either. I really don't know if that was the reason, but to my thinking, it did figure in on it!

Oh, by the way, Uncle Tom said Houston wasn't drinking that night!

Uncle Drew

By Homer C. Ledford

One would never forget a man like him—
Uncle Drew Ledbetter.
He lived by the "code of the mountains."
His fist was of the highest steel.
His eyes would penetrate the toughest stone,
Looking out from under the eyebrows
That remind one of the
Sassafras hedges that grew along his farm.

UNCLE DREW was getting along in years,
Ninety years young to be exact.
He was stooped in stature and walked with a limp,
But he would walk that extra mile
Just to play a prank on the unsuspected.

Oversized overalls was his dress.
Everyday and Sunday too.
A proud man, an honest man,
A solid citizen!
A lot can be learned from such a man
As Uncle Drew.

He had character,
Strength of will
Fearlessness,
And a very strong desire
To help his fellow man.

UNCLE DREW HAD A HEART OF GOLD!

I peer out of the windows near where I sat during my days at the one-room Ivy Point School.

Ivy Point School

If you were going from my house to Ivy Point School, it would take you down across a little creek, over across our pasture field just above Uncle Bugg's house, up through the Ferrell Cemetery to the main dirt road around about another half mile to Uncle Tom's house, down across the foot-log across Cowan Branch, and finally a short walk on the path nearly straight up to the school.

There it sat, a huge building by local standards. It sported a large bell tower on top of the roof, which housed one of the finest bells in the state. The roof was made of wooden shingles, and all the siding was yellow poplar weather boarding, which was originally painted white. Years of weathering and no fresh paint had turned it to a more grayish color.

There were six windows on each side, two at one end and only the door at the other. It was heated by an old pot-bellied wood burning stove. That sure was great in the winter time. We just gathered around it and stuck our feet up as close as we could get, which wasn't too close, because there were too many of us. It's hard to get twenty kids and one teacher very close. You weren't going to get burned by touching it, I can tell you that!

The floor was something else. It was made of rough planking straight from the local saw mill. There was some attempt by my uncle Ben McDonald, who was a carpenter, to plane some of the roughness off. Eventually, there would be so much mud and dirt carried in that it was necessary to treat the floor with something that would keep the dust down. That dust would be unhealthy, you know. So Uncle Ben and some of the other "brains" around there came up with an idea. They went into town and got a five-gallon bucket full of burned black motor oil. They waited until Friday came and got us boys to help and pour that oil all over that floor. What a mess! It did keep the dust down, but there was another advantage. We found we could skate on that oil slick floor if we would put our shoes on. We didn't need splinters in our feet, you know.

So here we went. We would take a "running shoot" and hit that floor like gang busters! Let me tell you though—I'm afraid I played it to the limits and beyond—because one of my shoes came untied and came off just as I hit those black planks. There was a splinter in one of those boards and it tore right into my foot. That splinter felt big enough to make a bunch of over-sized tooth picks. To say I was in pain was the understatement of the year. Uncle Ben took me home and mother, she was so loving, poured turpentine on it, smeared on Cloverine salve, and bandaged it up. It did the trick, apparently, since I am still here!

I learned a lot in that old school house. Some of it was book learning, but some was learning how to fight and ride bicycles. Well, I also learned how to cuss, but I never put it into practice. Mother and Dad made me not want to. If I had and Mother and Dad had found out about it, I would have been a dead duck.

All eight grades was taught in the one room so we could hear what was going on with the class before us. It helped prepare us for the next grade also. Another advantage was there were three black boards on the walls on which to put your arithmetic, songs, spelling words or what have you. I learned my multiplication, addition, and subtraction tables that way.

When the teacher needed to change classes, he would ring his little bell, which he always kept right near him on the desk. He also used that bell to announce recess. We always had morning, dinner, and evening recess. Of course that is when we got our extracurricular education. We played town ball, which was mostly taking a sponge rubber ball and batting the dickens out of it and running around the three bases. Another favorite was "fox and hound." We usually had two hounds and a bunch of foxes. The creeks, hills and bluffs came in real handy for that game.

A very interesting item was the "privy" or toilet. We didn't have inside plumbing. At first we didn't even have the privy. There were always plenty of trees and bluffs nearby. The state finally decided that all schools must have a toilet and so they sent their mighty fine carpenters and materials and erected a prize winner. Actually there were two built because the girls needed one too.

The new toilets presented a problem for the teacher. Everybody wanted to use it whether they needed to or not. We would just about stand in line to get to use it. This eventually became quite troublesome for him, so he finally figured out a scheme. He made us hold our hands up, come up to his desk, and sign his little black book. I don't recall having to put any "whys" down. I was told that came later.

So I spent eight years in that one room school house. I was all educated to the level I was supposed to be and eventually was ready for high school. I sure hated to leave that place. A lot of good memories are burned in my mind forever!

Ivy Point School sat close to the road in front, but behind the school house was a cliff that dropped into the creek. The children were not allowed to go near to the precipice. It was an exciting day when the privy was built behind the school house.

If I Could Only Be Little Again

by Julia (Ledford) Baker

If I could only be little again
The world to experience, my life to begin
Nature, a canvas for me to paint on
Myself a soft flower for nature to don.

With ever fresh eagerness, ready to flaunt
A crinkly grin, and form so gaunt
Mud-caked fingers, wind-bent hair
And naked feet without a care.

Running with laughter, 'til day becomes night
And the dew sifts down where fireflies light
The pink glimmer of day came never too soon
Before I, with the birds would sing a glad tune.

The sunshine above, and plant life beneath
In between me, making green clover wreaths
Now time has flown by, and beckons me in
If only I could be little again.

Above, from left, are our daughters Julie and Cindy and their friend, Tammy Tarkington.

The Old Wagon Road Between Home and School

I was just a little "pup," but I remember well walking along on some of the "cow paths" and wagon roads in the foothills of the Cumberland Mountains in Tennessee where I was born and reared. In particular, there was the road leading from my house to the little one-room school a little over a mile away.

My walk to school took me by Uncle Bugg's house just across the pasture, through the graveyard just above Uncle Bugg's house, and split the middle of the big corn field belonging to my uncle Tom Ledford. Next, it went right by Uncle Tom's house on the hill and down across the little Cowan Branch near to the footlog crossing just below the road. Up the very steep hill, it made the last turn and right there I was, standing in front of the little Ivyton Elementary School, where I spent eight years trying to get some education.

There were usually two, three, or even four of us kids that had to walk that old road coming home from school each evening. After school everybody was just about starved, having played and studied so hard, so we would eat just about anything to satisfy that craving.

In the fall there were lots of wild grapes, 'possum grapes as we called them, growing in the woods. So we went across over to Uncle Tom's woods which were right along the road, and climbed the big hickory tree where the wild grape vines full of fruit had twisted themselves all around the branches. Boy, did we feast! The problem was, we over did it. We ate so many of those grapes that it created a real pressing health problem. Yes, we really had to go! There was no question about it either; we did not make it home before nature had it's way!

We also learned another lesson. We found it didn't pay to go by Mr. Smith's apple orchard and eat those green apples either. Not only did we have to "go" a lot, but you'd think we had been kissing our sweethearts the way our mouths and lips were "puckered."

The 'simmon trees alongside that road also furnished some good "puckering" fruit also. We came to learn that it was best to let the 'possoms have the persimmons. There just wasn't much future in eating those things, especially when they were only half-ripe!

The Fight

Things weren't always so smooth for me either as I jour neyed along that old road. I'll never forget a fighting experience I had coming from school one evening. My two brothers, Paul and J.B., were with me as well as the local bully, a boy named Smith. He was always trying to "pick" on me, trying to raise a fight. He knew I was too small to be a match for him.

Coming up the hill just below Uncle Tom's house, he was pushing me around and trying to put dirt on me, and finally, I got fed up with it. I knew I couldn't do much with my fists, but it just flew all over me. So, I reached down and found an "equalizer," a nice flat stone weighing about a half a pound and threw it at him. When that thing connected, Smith came to the conclusion the fight was over. He never bothered me again. Yes, I was thankful that road had plenty of rocks around!

Falling in the Ice-Covered Creek

It was in the middle of winter and was very cold with lots of ice and snow on the ground. That's the way it was that morning when I came to the old footlog crossing the creek. I started to cross over it, but when i got about halfway across, I decided to linger a little longer and throw a few pebbles in the creek and watch them glide across the ice to the other side.

The footlog was built so that it had some planks nailed down on it, making it flat and easier to walk on without falling off. Well, there were some extra planks turned at right angles to it, and I thought I would get out on the end of one of those so I could get a better shot at the ice across on the other side. I had selected a pretty good sized flat rock, made a right handed throw with that thing and down I went with it! I crashed right through the ice, making a hole just the shape of my body. Boy, was that water cold!

It didn't take me near as long to make the trip up to Uncle Tom's house as it used to! Aunt Verlie found some of cousin Charles' clothes for me to wear. Trouble was, they were a little oversized for me, and I would have to take two steps before they would catch up with me! I kinda' wished that old road hadn't led to the creek!

Crossing the Raging Creek

The Cowan branch that ran just below our school had a bad habit of "getting up" when the rains came. Way up the creek, the mountains and hills came down on both sides of the creek, making a funnel that fed all the water into the creek and, of course, making it wild and swift. It became wilder than a "touched rabbit!"

On this particular day, I was in school that day when a big thunderstorm came, washing out the footlog and leaving me no way to get home. It wasn't too long before Dad and Mom became very worried about me and she made Dad get on the old mule and come looking for me. I had come down to the swollen creek just to wait for it to go down, and also to watch the interesting items go floating by such as shoes, clothes, old cans and even one old outdoor plumbing item.

Well, finally, here came Dad on top of the old red, long-legged mule named Tobe. That sure was a welcome sight. Dad was what we called short and dumpy, not skinny like me. His legs wouldn't reach down far enough to wrap them around the mule. That concerned me considerably. I was afraid he would fall off. He did have a saddle, however, and looked like he was going to make it across the swollen creek okay. He made it across just fine, but now the problem was getting me on the mule behind him. We looked around and finally found a stump nearby and Dad maneuvered Tobe up to it and I jumped on behind Dad from there. We made it back across, but needless to say, I was scared nearly half to death.

I just wished that school house would have been on the other side of the creek. We never did need to cross that creek all swollen like that again though. At least, I am still here!

The Old Road Home

By Homer C. Ledford

There are numerous roads
we have traveled in our lives.
Some have taken us to
fabulous places, huge cities.
And some have taken us to
places that bear sadness,
tragedy.

But there is one road
We cherish more than all
And that is
THE OLD ROAD TO HOME.

Rough, crooked, hilly, mud
holes but it brings us back.
Good memories
of relatives, friends
and neighbors
along the way.

No matter which road we
choose, the bad ones,
the good ones.
In our minds we can choose
for all roads to be good.
And these roads will all be
THE OLD ROAD TO HOME

The Vaccinations

In my community of Ivyton, Tennessee, which was later changed to Alpine, Tennessee, we had no doctors to go to when we became ill. The closest one was in Livingston some twelve miles away, a great distance when we had no way of getting there except by walking or riding a mule and that was just about out of the question. My uncle, Abe Copeland, had a car, but you had to walk a rough three miles or more to get to his house. He was the one that owned the grocery store where we shopped regularly.

When it was time for a baby to be born, the birth was taken care of either by a "midwife" or you'd get someone to go over to Uncle Abe's store and call the doctor from there. Uncle Abe also was the only one that had a phone at that time. The doctor would come as far as he could by car, which was within about three miles usually. Then someone, a friend, relative or the daddy, would take a mule and fetch him the rest of the way. Sometimes the baby would beat the doctor there!

Finally, Overton County began to get a little money from the state to help out with setting up a health department. It was very limited, but was a start. About the only thing they could do was hire a health nurse to go into the schools and conduct limited examinations such as checking for bad teeth, poor eyesight, tape worms and many other ailments commonly found in the mountain communities such as ours.

One of the best programs established by the health department was providing inoculations for typhoid, and smallpox. The nurse would ride a horse and go around to all the schools in our area. This was quite a task, but thank goodness she only had to do this twice a year, and sometimes only once a year depending on conditions in the community and the weather.

I remember the first time the announcement came that we were to get our shots. A lot of folks around there just about panicked. They had heard that some folks had died from having the typhoid shots, and they were not about to let them vaccinate their children. They kept them away from school since that was where the shots were to be given. Most folks around there had no education and didn't understand anything about inoculations. There was no way of enforcing the ruling, so some kids had to go unprotected.

Our inoculation station was set up in our little Ivyton School. That made it more convenient for most of the folks around there. It came time for us all to be "protected" and it was our time, meaning my sister Gladys, J.B., Paul, and me. We were starting to line up, but then we noticed one of us was absent. They got to checking and found J.B. had run off and hid under the floor. They tried and tried to get him out, but the floor was too close to the ground and only J.B. could get under there. They finally got him out and vaccinated him, but only after offering him candy and a new pair of shoes.

Needles used today are much shorter, but boy back then they seemed like they were two inches long! The nurse would take that long needle, push it into the vial of serum which had what looked like a rubber disc fitted over the end, pull it out full of serum, hold it vertically and squirt some out to make sure no air bubbles were present. No wonder J.B. ran because even I thought that needle would go all the way through my arm!

They sterilized the needles by putting them in a pan of boiling water. This way they could use them over and over again. Not the best way to guarantee they were sterile, but the only way they had in those days. We have come a long way since then. Everything is perfect now!

One year the nurse didn't come to the schools. They made us go into town instead. We had to meet at the school to catch a big one and one-half ton truck. That was some experience! The truck was closed in to protect us from the weather and from falling off. They put about fifteen of us on that thing and here we went. You haven't lived until you have traveled to Livingston on those crooked roads up Alpine Mountain in that old truck. When we went around those crooked, steep curves, we would lean one way just to find the truck had already headed the other way. We felt like a bunch of cattle headed to the market.

When we arrived, they lined us up and started "squirting and stabbing." They ran us through in no time flat!

Well, folks, I guess we were adequately protected because no one caught the diseases we were vaccinated against. At least none that I know of!

Thin Ice

We had some great times in and around that little one-room school. You see it sat right on top of the hill above the creek known as Cowan Branch. The little creek wound it's way about four or five miles down to West Fork River. A lot of good times could be had around that creek.

In those days we would get out for recess thirty minutes in mid-morning, one hour for lunch or dinner as we called it, and thirty minutes mid-afternoon. We had lots of time to get into trouble since the teacher never supervised our "activities" very much. I guess she had her own thing to do like sleeping!

The creek was frozen over that winter and we spent our recess time going down to the creek and skating across it where it was the widest. It was probably about thirty feet across. We didn't have regular skates, just our high top "brogan" shoes, which most of the time had holes in the soles. We would go up to the top of the hill, oh, about a good fifty feet or more, take a running shoot and hit that ice like gang busters! Boy what a thrill!

Well, I was going to be "Big Ike" and try something bigger than everyone else. I went way back on the hill, took a fast running shoot and hit that ice with all "four feet!" One little detail I didn't consider, the weather had warmed up just enough to melt some of the ice on the other side. With me having no brakes and being unable to negotiate a stop, I went right through the ice where it was about knee deep to a duck. Boy, was it cold!

The boys got me up to the school house and put me beside the old wood burning stove and dried me out. I figured the teacher would warp my frame, but no, I guess she thought I had been punished enough, and I would not argue with that.

I don't recollect ever getting on that ice again without checking out the holes first!

Uncle Bugg's house was once full of activity and life. Though vacant now, it still stands on Black Hollow Road.

The Picture

By Homer C. Ledford

His picture hung on the wall
Above the corn shuck bed
That he used to sleep on.
I loved to look at that picture
The kindest eyes—loving.

Hair parted arrow straight
Right down the middle of his head.
Beard flowed down over
The pearl buttons on his shirt.

I thought he was looking at me,
Trying to tell me something.
Son, you must carry on
And always do what is right
In your heart.

I think a lot about that picture
I see a great man here,
A peaceful man.
One that loved his family,
His neighbor.

Strong willed,
Never gave way to evil.
Yes, that picture tells me a lot-
Yet, I really never had the privilege
To talk with him
Before he passed on.

But I knew him well, anyway.
Because he was my grandfather!
"Uncle Jim McDonald."

My parents were buried in the Ferrell Cemetery near our homeplace in Overton County, Tennessee.

Otis Gets Even with Dinah

Uncle Otis McDonald was not much on getting upset or angry. As a matter of fact, most folks could get upset in a whiz, where it took Uncle Otis five to ten minutes to do it. Otis moved slowly by nature, but could get the job done if you were willing to wait. I never saw Uncle Otis angry in my whole life. However, I am sure he must have because Grandma, his mother, whom he stayed with, said he did, but it was rare.

I acutely remember this one time when Uncle Otis was plowing his corn with his old mule Dinah. Dinah was short for dynamite. He had a big field of corn, nice and green. It had been rained on well and everything.

"Mighty nice to have a crop like that," Otis said. "Yes, the only trouble was getting it plowed at the right time and 'laying it by'."

The rows of corn must have been one quarter mile long and there were lots of rows so Otis had plenty of time to get frustrated. So he did!

I just happened to be coming through the graveyard that day, close to where Otis was plowing. I was on my way home from the post office. I was expecting my new guitar to come in. From this vantage point, I could see where he was plowing, but just couldn't see him yet. There was a bunch of sassafras bushes there that were blocking my view. All of a sudden, out popped Otis and Dinah from behind those bushes, taking off like a "bat out of Ivyton." He was slapping that mule with his check lines like crazy and looked like he was shouting some real "heavy" words. I know Otis wasn't the cussing type, but I believe in my heart that he was coming mighty close!

Later, Otis and I were talking and I asked, "What in the world was going on that day?"

He said, "Homer, that crazy mule would slow down after making the turn at the end, and then when we got to the end of the row, he would speed up, do a quick turn and cause me to plow up a good fifty to one hundred hills of corn. That went on for I don't know how long and I had just had enough of that, don't you know! So I decided, Ole Gal you're gonna pay for that!"

The only thing was, from what I could see, Uncle Otis was paying more than Dinah! She was literally pulling him across the field with no effort on her part at all. He was just barely holding onto the plow handles and it looked like both feet were doing more plowing than the plow was. The dust was flying, the corn rows were parting, and it reminded me more of a hurricane!

When it all settled down in my mind, I thought Uncle Otis was getting punished more than the mule. But, if Uncle Otis says he got even, he got even! End of story!

From left, my brother Paul and I pose with Uncle Otis and our first instruments, a mail order guitar and mandolin. The only mandolin we had seen was in a catalog, so when it arrived it was smaller than we expected and Paul didn't want it. It suited me just fine.

Learning to Milk
Or Trying To

Have you ever tried to milk a cow when you were thirteen-years-old, especially if you didn't want to in the first place?

Let me tell you about my experience.

Dad most always had two cows and they were not the kind that gave lots and lots of milk. I never thought they gave the milk. I thought you had to take it. He was always trading for the kind of cows the folks around there called "hard teats", meaning they were very hard to milk. I was used to peeking through the cracks to watch Dad do the milking, but I never thought that I would want to do it. I remember there were times when Dad would aim the stream of milk at me through the cracks of the barn. He'd try to hit me right in the face with it. Sometimes he hit his mark. I didn't like that too well.

One day Dad said, "Homer, it is time for you to learn to milk the cows and I won't have to do it myself. You can get up at 6:00 o'clock in the morning and get that all done while I'm doing the other feeding and ginning." Getting up that early in the morning didn't appeal to me a bit. You see, I was what they called a genuine sleepy head.

Well, he took me out to the barn, reached me the milk bucket and said, "Kneel down right here beside the old girl and I'll walk you through it." I did what he said, trying to be cooperative, you know. "Now you see here, there are four teats and that is where the milk is."

I understood that part fine.

"Now take your hand, grip with the top of your hand first, then squeeze the bottom and the milk will just come a flying!"

I tried to do just that. I put my hand up just like he said and started to squeeze. I mean I squeezed hard with all my grip and about that time old "Blackie," that was the cow's name cause she was black I guess, picked up that back leg and with a forward kick, landed me over in the manure! Not a good sight! Dad said, "Son let me see those fingers. Well, no wonder the old gal kicked you, your finger nails look like they are one inch long. You almost stabbed that poor cow with those things. She just doesn't take to that too hot."

I whipped out my pocket knife and did a trim job on my nails and now I was ready to do the job right this time. "Now son, do as I said before and you'll have no problem."

I did and that stream of milk hit the bottom of that bucket screaming out a "B flat" if I ever heard one!.

I did a few squirts like that and WHAMMO, that old cow let me have it right across the face with that big long bushy tail. What made it even worse that tail had been in I don't know what all—hay, manure, cockle burrs and Spanish needles. Needless to say, I fell back spilling what milk I had managed to extract from old Blackie and just felt plumb like a complete failure.

"Homer, you're hopeless. You're just like that old man across the creek over there—dumb, dumb, dumb!"

Now that hurt to the quick! He said I could take my pocket knife and whittle, carry water for Mother and a few other things he felt I could do and would never have to milk the cows again.

To this day and this is a long piece down the road, I have never milked a cow and don't ever expect to! I'd much rather squeeze the neck of a guitar, banjo or fiddle. Now, wouldn't you?

My First Time to Shoot a Shotgun

M y older brother Paul and I were sitting on the front porch swing just taking it easy after a day in the field plowing and hoeing corn, when all of a sudden Paul said, "Domer, (Domer was what he gave me for a nickname and I didn't like it a bit.) it's about time I taught you how to shoot a shotgun."

"Paul, I've been telling you I don't like shotguns. They make too much noise, kick like a wild mule, and besides, I like my twenty-two rifle which serves me just fine."

However, Paul insisted, "You're gonna have to learn it sooner or later, so lets go."

After thinking on it a few minutes, I finally gave in.

The only shotgun in sight was Dad's old twelve-gauge. Now that's a big shotgun. They always said that thing would be so loud when it went off you could almost be heard way over in the next county. Dad never did know much about fixing things around the place and that shotgun was no exception. The stock, the wooden part you hold against your shoulder, was very loose and seemed to me like almost ready to fall off. When a shotgun has a loose stock like that, it makes it kick (recoil) harder than a wild mule. Whatever, that gun was most likely to kill in front and cripple behind!

Well, reluctantly, I grabbed the gun and Paul and I headed on down over the hill, across the little creek, and up the other side to the cow pasture where Paul said we were most likely to "jump" a rabbit.

We came upon a good sized patch of blackberry briars, and Paul threw a rock into them to scare the rabbit out. Sure enough, out ran a big old cottontail.

Paul yelled, "Shoot, Domer, shoot."

I pulled the hammer back on that cannon, put it to my shoulder, aimed in the general direction of the rabbit and jerked that trigger like a pro. BOOM!!! That gun went off, and that stock tore into my shoulder like a sledge hammer on a railroad spike! It almost laid me down right there, and on top of that, my ears were ringing something terrible!

Let me tell you right now that rabbit was a lot safer in front of my gun barrel than he was running under the barbed wire fence he squeezed through!

Paul laughingly said, "Now Domer, wasn't that a real experience?"

And I angrily responded, "Paul, you talked me into shooting that dad blamed gun this time, but I will never, never, never, shoot a shotgun again!"

And I haven't!

The Overton County courthouse in Livingston, Tennessee, sits on a town-square where the Ledfords visited only on special occasions. Sometimes on weekends we played music in the second floor courtroom for anyone who would listen.

The Silent Movie

Good solid, decent "G" rated entertainment was hard to come by in the little community of Ivyton, Tennessee, where I was born and raised. A lot of folks would entertain themselves by getting drunk on "white lightning," fighting, or having "shoot outs." Most of us were kinfolks, and didn't take to that kind of thing. It just was not good for the health, you know.

We had our churches to go to, a "pie supper" now and then where they would auction off some of the best chocolate pies and layer cakes that were all covered with icing and looked ever bit of six to eight inches high! The girls would bring them and, of course, hoped the most handsome boy would buy theirs. Unfortunately, I never had any money, and besides I was lacking on the handsome side!

We also had spelling bees in the old school house. Sometimes they had small cash prizes for the best speller. I outspelled them one time, but there was no money in it. Just my luck! Well that was about it for entertainment, unless you wanted to play Rook, Checkers, or have a "cotton pickin" good time picking cotton seeds out of the cotton we raised on the farm.

This one time word got out that there was going to be a movie shown in our old school house on a Friday night after school. Needless to say, the whole neighborhood was overcome with excitement—me too! We had never seen a movie before, or for that matter, I don't recall hearing about one. This was gonna be a biggie.

Saturday arrived and so did the movie crew. I had never seen anything like it. They traveled in an old Model-T Ford, a big two seater! The school had no electricity, so the movie crew brought their own. I want you to know they jacked that old Model-T up, raising both back wheels off the ground so they could turn freely, and took one wheel off, exposing just the round brake drum. They had a generator mounted on a large bench so it would be solid, and attached a flat belt from the generator to the car wheel to generate enough power to run the movie machine. You know, I would have paid money, if I had it, just to see that contraption!

Everything was going fine until the movie fellers figured they would have to hang blinds on the windows so the ones that didn't get a ticket couldn't see the movie.

Well that didn't set too well with the local bully. Everybody knew him as Ez. I reckon that was short for Ezra. Well, Ez told the movie fellers, "You can't do that son. We gotta' see that movie too and we ain't paying a plug nickel!"

That took care of that then and there. The window blinds were taken down and things settled down pretty calm after that.

The movie was a silent western. You ask me how could you tell what they said if it was silent. Well, they put the words on the screen so you could read what was going on. Boy, it sure was a wild show. Lots of shooting, riding up and down mountains, crossing impossible streams and creating all kinds of action. Like the rest, I was literally sitting on the edge of my seat! We were "petrified," or I think that is the word.

I sure would like to see one of those silent movies today—in HI FI! Dream on Homer!

Uncle Otis's Stolen Trap

In my neck of the woods down there in the mountains of Central Tennessee, just about everybody loved to trap for fur, skunks, 'possums, foxes and the like. The hills and rivers in Overton County were just right for good trappin'.

Uncle Otis was no different from the rest of the natives around there. He set out a lot of steel traps over those hills and right below his little cabin.

One morning it was time for him to go to check his traps, so he walked on down over the swag into a little ravine where he had this particularly big trap. He knew he just had to have a big fox in it. Well, lo and behold, he had just stepped out around the bluff of rock and there he was, another feller was already down there where his trap was supposed to be. Otis never was one to jump right into anything he didn't know that much about, so, he politely hid behind the nearest tree to watch what he was doing.

Right there before his very own eyes something was happening he'd never dreamed of. The guy was putting Uncle Otis' steel trap in the leg of his overalls. Uncle Otis got to thinking pretty serious on it, and had taken in about all of this he could stand. So, he eased on down to the feller and asked him, "Have you seen my trap down this way?"

The feller replied, "Why, no, I shore haint. Why do you ask?"

About that time ole Otis shook the feller's britches leg real hard and out came the trap!

His reply was, "Well, how in the worl' did that thing get in thar?"

Uncle Otis said, "You know, it don't git you nowhere to steal a feller's steel trap!"

I reckon trapping went smoother after that. At least I never heard him complain again.

Upside Down Turnips
(Fictitious)

It wasn't everybody in the mountains of Tennessee where I grew up who was so endowed with smartness. As a matter of fact, there were a few that we could say weren't "going up with a full load!" I knew one of them.

I am gonna give him a nickname, Cedric, just to protect the guilty. Cedric was the kind that you could send for the cows in the pasture, and he would bring back a couple of chickens he had stolen from my uncle. Yes, he was some character.

He never did like cucumbers, bell peppers and the like and especially let us know he would not touch turnip greens. I said, "Cedric, why in the world don't you like turnip greens?"

"Homer, I just don't like 'going' that often. Boy, for some reason I'm an easy touch along that line. It's terrible!"

"Cedric, do you like the turnips themselves?"

"Yes, I love them."

"Well, what have you done about it?"

"I simply go and get me some seed and plant them up side down."

"And that works?"

"No, not yet, but you know what, I am going to try the young sprouts by setting the tops down first. I think I'm on to it now, don't you?"

I'm not what you'd call a "bright star" either, but I figured out that twasn't ever goin to work. What do you think?

Alone After Dark

I love to play music very much. I just happened to be at the right place at the right time, but unfortunately, I took this job to do by myself. I told the folks in the square dance troop that I would play for their square dance down at the Standing Stone State Park near Livingston, Tennessee, twelve miles from where I lived.

Clarence Ferrell, the leader of the dance group, said they would come pick me up if I would meet them down at the old concrete bridge about a mile below my house. I said I would. We went on down to the park and I played for about two good hours and then it came time to go home. As it turned out, it was about midnight when we arrived at the old river bridge where he was to let me off. I had a little flashlight with me that I had bought in town when Dad and I went Christmas shopping, and I thought that would get me home. I followed the old wagon road to the top of the hill, which wasn't too bad, but the trouble was, I had another good mile to go before reaching the safety of home. I knew the going would be tougher after that.

It so happened when you reached the top of the hill, there was an old abandoned house right on the path and I had to pass right by it. All of the windows and doors were missing and it just looked real scary. In fact, all the folks around there said it was haunted. Well, I was just about to reach the haunted house when, lo and behold, my flashlight conked out. Yep, quit shining completely. It was as dark as the inside of a black cat! I managed to shake myself up even with the house and just about that time, I heard the weirdest, wildest sound coming right from the house! Now, if my feet never wanted to move fast before, they did at that time! I hardly knew which way to go, but the best route seemed to be by the fence row that I knew was located above the house. But, POW! I ran right into the fence and it bounced me back like a rubber band. Finally with all my strength, I took a "running shoot" and jumped that four-foot high fence and had some room to spare, don't you know!

Well, I followed the fence on up to Grandma's house, cut across Uncle Otis' corn patch and finally made it to my house and safety. I think I made a thirty minute trip in less than ten minutes. One thing I do know, if you are scared enough, you will cover a whole lot more ground!

Down a steep hill from our home was the West Fork River. Only the support cables remain from a swinging bridge that was the family's means of crossing.

The Falling into the River Caper

Otis McDonald was just one of my favorite uncles. He spoke somewhat slowly and with what we called a "Southern drawl." If you had plenty of time, he sure could tell you some mighty interesting and funny stories, and I think that they all were true.

Well, Otis and I were sitting around the old fireplace one evening and the subject came up about fishing, which Otis really, really loved to do. Otis said, "I'm gonna' tell you just what happened to a friend of mine back in the summer. You see, my friend Jim had slipped down to the river there to do a little fishin' and kinda' had a little bad luck. He was reaching up to pull a little sprout to make a fishin' pole, it broke, and Jim fell right into the river where it was about waist deep, pole and all. It didn't hurt him one bit, according to Jim. Don't you know, I found that hard to believe and told Jim of it." Jim said, 'I'll take you right down to where I fell in and show you the place and prove it.' I said, "Let's go and since I didn't have much else to do, we struck out."

We went back down to the river and right above the deepest hole where he said he had fallen before. Jim said, "Now this is exactly the way I did it." He pulled and pulled on the little sapling that stood there, and don't you know it broke and sent ole Jim right back down in the water just like before! And it didn't hurt him this time either!

Otis allowed as how, "I reckon it takes a plumb fool to do such a thing and not get a scratch!"

Getting Higher Than a Kite

Moonshine, white lightning, rot-gut likker were very common terms down around where I'm from in the mountains of North Central Tennessee. The favorite pastime was getting dog drunk or trying to shoot up the local hangout on Saturday night. We didn't have anything going on like that in our community, but up the West Fork River about five or six miles from us, there were some mining towns scattered along Route 85. There wasn't any law enforcement up there so the natives just took the law into their own hands. It just didn't seem to matter what they did, good or bad.

Speaking of moonshine and such, I'm just gonna' tell you about what happened to my Uncle Otis.

Otis definitely was not the drinking kind, and according to him, never took a drop in his life. I guess that was bound to change eventually. So it did!

The way it happened was, one Sunday afternoon a couple of Otis' friends came by and wanted him to go with them up to the church, which was about a mile nearly straight up the mountain. A revival meeting was going on up there and the fellers allowed as how Uncle Otis ought to take in some of it. Now this is where it gets kinda' interesting.

One of the fellers said, "Otis, we got a little "toddy" (likker) around here behind the chimney and think we ought to have a little swig just to get us all "braced up" good for the journey. It's a good ways up that Kings Mountain where the church is."

Otis said, "I never drunk a drop in my life and I don't know what kind of effect it would have on me. I'm just plain 'skittish' of it fellers."

"Oh, come on, we do it all the time and look at us."

"Well, might as well try it."

Black Hollow Road ends at the Ledford homeplace.

Ole Otis took that pint jar, which by the way was nearly full of the "tonic," put it to his mouth, and drank about half of it, and according to Otis, lit up like a Christmas tree!

Well, Otis was doing fine until they got about half way up the mountain, and then it hit him like a sledge-hammer!

"You fellers go on up and I'll just sit here on this stump 'til my brother comes down to get me."

No sooner had he got on the stump 'til he fell right off backward. He repeated these tumbles three or four times and was beginning to get a little tired of that, if you know what I mean.

Soon his brother, Uncle Ben McDonald, came down and drug him up to the church house and began to feed him up on cheese and crackers to sober him up. They said he consumed one whole pound of cheese and a box of Saltines. My notion here is that's enough to sober you up or kill you, or both!

Otis declared, "I will never do the white lightnin' thing again, and will never, never like cheese and crackers again!! And he didn't! Can't say I blame him one bit.

Jim

This is about Jim—Jim Shumate. Jim was a big tall fellow with unusually long arms and legs. Why his hands hung down below his shirt sleeves a good four inches. His legs extended way below the bottom of his overall legs. It looked like he had cut his britches legs off three times, but they were still too short. Jim was getting older now and his skin was very dark and wrinkled. The sun and age will do that to you sometimes. When he looked at you, it gave you the feeling he was mean and tough—and he was! Folks around said he would "fight a circle saw."

I think the environment where Jim grew up had a great deal to do with how he was. From my house you had to walk a mile to the post office and as if that wasn't bad enough, you had to go another mile through the woods on a path that took you down across a kind of ravine, across a small creek on a foot-log which was used as a bridge, up the hill another half mile past what we knew as the old saltpeter cave, and we were finally there. His house was just a log structure with two rooms, one window and a front and back door. Oh yes, there was a chimney to accommodate the wood burning fireplace. I'm here to tell you, Jim lived in the "boonies!" His wife had passed on so he had his dog, ole Benjamin (Ben for short), to keep him company and help him with hunting his game.

People liked ole Jim and feared him at the same time. Sometimes they would look in on him just to see if everything was ok.

Jim liked to travel around, not long distances, just places he could walk to. But sometimes he would have a hankering to go downtown about twelve miles away. He had no car or even a mule so he would walk to the highway, which was really a gravel road, and thumb (hitch-hike) a ride to town. There was a great danger in this for Jim, but he didn't seem to grasp it all too well. He would get right out in the middle of the road, stick his arm straight out, thumb pointing to the sky and yell, "stop!" It usually worked. They about had to stop or run over him, you know.

People kept telling him he was going to get killed if he didn't stop gettin' into the middle of the road like that. Well, time passed and he went on thumbing and one day it happened. It was foggy and there Jim was, right in the middle of the road almost invisible to traffic and it happened! I hate to tell you but he got exactly what the folks predicted.

Jim was sadly missed. He really did help folks out when he could. He was a hard worker and believed in doing the right things by his neighbors.

The Moonshine Still
Up the Holler

B ack in my young days when I was just a little "sprout," there was a lot of illegal whiskey being made. Those hollows around there were full of it. All you had to have was a nice little cave, or some hollow and a clear running spring, a still, and you were in business. Of course there had to be privacy and that sure wasn't a problem with the locals, certainly not with us because we always tried to mind our own business, you see.

Well, right across the little creek from us was a wagon road that led right up to the mountain and ended there. This was about a mile and a half up there and a perfect spot for making "white lightnin'."

There were some enterprising young fellers that lived up that way and had set up business. Most everybody knew about it, but never said a word to anybody, especially to the authorities. It would have been very dangerous to rat on these moonshiners because we had heard they had a bad habit of shooting first and asking questions later. That could have been very bad for one's health! Anyway, most of the folks around there except us, enjoyed the fruits of their labor. Man, the "buzzards in the sky got so drunk they couldn't fly" smelling that stuff!

Things were going pretty good for the boys until one day the county decided to run a grader up that way and make the road passable for the Model-T Ford cars. Now that the road was in good shape for automobiles, it made it risky business to run a moonshine still. I'll never forget that little spindly trail of smoke as it reached for the sky as if to tell us things were going great up there. It was so regular that you could about set your watch by it!

One day an unfamiliar sound reached our ears and it was progressing right up the little crooked road leading up to the foot of the mountain. We just couldn't believe our ears, but it was an old Model-T Ford car winding it's way up to the end of the trail. Well, we got to figuring and came up with boy that has to be the revenuers, and yes, that little spindly smoke from that little endeavor up there was no more! They had finally found the boys and shut them down!

Well, I figure the big mistake the boys made was that they forgot to close the big iron gate at the end of the road, and, they apparently didn't have their "Peacemakers" with them that day either.

White lightning making was slowed down to a crawl after that, but I did hear later that the operations had moved across the mountain where only a mule could go or you had to hoof it yourself!

My First Date

I wasn't going to tell this on myself, but I got to thinking on it and thought, "Oh, what the heck! I'm older now, much older and it won't make that much difference anyhow."

There comes a time in a young boy's life, twelve- or thirteen-years-old, or somewhere in there, when the girls begin to look a lot different, prettier, more interesting and several other things I can't think of right now.

Let me tell you what happened.

It was all very innocent to start out with. I didn't really have dating girls in mind. I was out at my Uncle Harris McDonald's house helping him build a barn. I think I was thirteen at the time. Uncle Harris had a son and daughter, Leslie and Lois, who were a little older than me and had some experience with the boys and girls. They were really beginning to get the "crazies" about the opposite sexes. I didn't have any experience along that line. I was oh so bashful! But I was beginning to get my wanting-to out ahead of everything else, don't you know!

One night the high school where Leslie and Lois was attending was putting on a stage play and Uncle Harris, Aunt Edna, Leslie, and Lois wanted me to attend it with them. Leslie said he wanted me to meet some of his girl friends. I was overcome with interest and went with them. They didn't need to beg me any, especially when they mentioned the pretty girls. Then it hit me! There was only one thing wrong. What in the world would I do if a girl sidled up to me real friendly like? Well, sure enough Leslie, knowing a lot of the girls there, introduced this beautiful little lady to me and, oh no, she seemed to take a liking to me. She even said, "Would you like to walk me home?" Oh boy, shock waves shot through my body like firecrackers in July! I couldn't figure out what in the world I was going to do! There were a whole lot of nays and ayes but the ayes won out and I said YES!

Now, it was about a mile to walk to her house, so we set out down the highway. It was dark as pitch and there was no light so we were obviously moving along slow and just feeling our way. I was very careful don't you know. I didn't want Trixie (Trixie Overstreet was her name, or nick name, and I never did really know her full name.) to fall down or anything. I was always considerate about those things.

Well, I'm going to tell you I was in for more surprises. We'd only gone about a half-mile when Trixie reached over and said, "Maybe you would be more comfortable if I held your hand." I said, "Uh-huh, that would be ok." And it was! Boy, was I living now. It was dark and nobody, especially not her, could see my bright red blush! You know when a person blushes that much, it can actually cause the darkness to light up a tad—and it did!!

A little further down the road a thought hit me somewhat hard. What if Leslie and the others had gone on home without me and I would have to "hoof" the three miles with these new shoes on which were now killing my feet. I hated to do it AND I was dreading like crazy what I would do if Trixie wanted to kiss me good night. But I pulled the big one anyway. I told her I needed to let her go on home alone as my family was going to go home without me. She almost had a kaniption fit, let loose my hand, and ran as fast as she could go, disappearing into the darkness! She never wanted to see me again. Can you blame her?

I guess I ruined that poor girl's life. I don't know what she is doing today. I guess we'll never know, will we?

My Physical for the Army

World war II was raging. Everybody in our parts was talking about the war effort. That is, what we could do to help out. Most of us were gathering up old scrap iron, donating cloth, cutting down on the use of coffee, sugar, or most
everything else it seemed. We were a very patriotic bunch and wanted to win that war mighty bad. We were about to get our chance, or at least I was, in a different way than I had ever dreamed of.

It wasn't long after my eighteenth birthday when I received a letter in the mail and on it were the big words, "GREETINGS from the U.S. Government." Oh, that letter sure looked very important. It was a nice tan color and from Washington, DC., no less.

I couldn't wait to open it since it was addressed to me. I tore that thing open, extracted that nicely folded letter and there it was. It read:

Mr. Homer C. Ledford
Ivyton, Tennessee

Dear Sir:
You are ordered to appear at your Local Board, Livingston, Tennessee, promptly at 8:00 a.m. on October 16, to be transported to Fort Oglethorpe, Georgia, the reception center, for your physical for the United States Army. Failure to do so will incur certain penalties which include............ If there should be circumstances that will prevent your presence, such as sickness, or death in the family, you may be excused, but you will have to fill out some forms as required by this office."

I almost had a heart attack! I knew I was of the age to go to the Army, but it really hadn't crossed my mind that they would ever find me up here in these mountains. I really did want to do my part to win this war, but picking up scrap metal was more my thing!

October 16 rolled around and Cousin Charles Ledford, myself and some other boys I knew from high school, boarded that old wreck of a bus and headed for Fort Oglethorpe, Georgia.

It was in the morning and I had very little sleep the night before worrying about it so I was pretty "shot" to start with.

After a four-hour ride over some of the roughest roads in Tennessee and Georgia, we finally arrived at our destination. We sure knew we were there when we spotted all the pup tents and long rectangular buildings called barracks. This sure didn't seem like home to me. No way!

First thing on the docket for us was to check in and fill out a stack of papers. I never did know what they all were for. I managed to get my full name down and home address. I was so scared that I almost forgot that! I'll never forget this one question, "Have you ever killed anyone?" I put, "NO!" I would have liked to have added, "And I don't intend to either!" I guess I was a little afraid to add anything. You never knew what they might do to you like slap you in the stockade maybe, and I SURE wanted to get back to my old familiar stomping ground, HOME!

By now it was chow time. We had to line up and I bet you that line was a half-mile long! They had plenty of food, but the only problem was I had no idea what any of it was except the chicken and a little piece of bread. Oh yes, I knew what the milk was. Boy, what I would have given for a big root beer and a deluxe hamburger about then!

After eating, we were assigned to our respective pup tents. There were four of us to a tent. The little cots were something else with hard mattresses lying on a plywood board, real luxury. The heater was a small pot bellied wood burning stove. Wouldn't you know it? It was cold that night and no wood to burn. A couple of the fellows said they weren't going to put up with that, so they lit out to find some. Here they came back with a couple of old benches they had found somewhere. I'm sure if the MP's had caught them, they would have been in deep trouble. They split them up by throwing them on the concrete floor and now we had enough for a good fire. At least that did the job for most of the night. I would have had some night mares except I didn't get to sleep long enough to have any. What a night!

The next morning found us all lined up again for BREAK-FAST! Now that word took on a different meaning when I focused my sleepy eyes on what they called breakfast. There weren't any of those good ole fried eggs, bacon, fluffy brown biscuits and coffee. I mean *real* coffee. Instead, the eggs turned out to be powdered? The biscuits were like shingles. I mean hard like the ones you use for roofing. The so-called bacon was a conglomeration of whatever was left over from another meal. The coffee tasted more like the bitters my Uncle Bugg McDonald concocted up from herbs, and it looked a lot like India ink.

Our appetites were pretty demanding at that hour so we made the most of it.

Our next assignment took us to a large room across the camp for a briefing. I thought, "What in the cat hair is a briefing?" We found out right away. The fellow in charge was a tough looking sergeant, and he looked like he wasn't one to put up with any foolishness. He wanted to know what condition our health was in. I don't think he learned much though, because very few questions were answered. I kept my mouth shut. I didn't want to incriminate myself on anything.

One reason I kept my mouth shut was this one guy spoke up and said he had ingrown toenails. The old sergeant broke out in such a hysterical laugh that I thought he was going to collapse right there! Then all the rest of the questionees joined in except me. I didn't think it was all that funny. Anyway, I was too scared to emote. No telling what that sarg would've done.

Now came the biggie. It was time for the physicals.

We were instructed to undress and line up down the hall-like room. The idea was to have us march before all these special doctors and get checked over to find out what was wrong with us, if anything. It was some sight to behold. There all of us were in our birthday suits all lined up down through there—some standard size, some way above standard and a few like me, skinny! I was really spooked out when I discovered one of the doctors was well, a female doctor! She checked our teeth, thank goodness! Now I was taught high modesty around women and this did not fit the bill. Right now I needed some fig leaves!

I made it through the various stations and finally arrived at the heart specialist. He listened to my pounding heart, and checked my pulse and my eyes. I don't know why the eyes. My eyes were so blood shot they looked like the road map of Georgia! Maybe that was it! He took my temperature, and I don't remember what all, but one thing I do remember, the doctor said, "Son, that heart will cause you to flunk the test. So he took that little ole rubber stamp he held in his hand and rammed it down so hard on my sheet. I'm sure you could hear it all way down the hall. Yes, I was REJECTED!

Now, the fact was, I didn't' want to have a defective heart, but I sure was glad I didn't have to go into the Army. That's just the way the cookie crumbles I guess.

The next morning after breakfast, a call come over the loud speaker for all who wanted to return home on the bus to gather out front in that big wide area next to Barracks II, pronto. We didn't want to miss that bus home so we lined up as commanded. SURPRISE! A voice came over the loud speaker saying, "Now everybody march across the area and pick up any trash you see. This includes cigarette butts, candy wrappers, chewing gum wrappers, or anything in your path." I didn't see anything for a while so I wasn't stooping any.

Then came another voice, "Hey you with that brown leather jacket on, (I was wearing a brown leather jacket alright.) get busy buster or you don't go home today!" You better believe it, I picked up a lot of things that weren't even there. Good grief, I didn't know he was watching so close!

Finally came the big moment. This time the call came that we would board our bus and head for home. We almost broke our necks running to get on that thing. That ride wasn't going to be nearly as bad going back home as it was going down to Georgia. And it wasn't!

This is the spring house Uncle Bugg built shortly after returning from World War I with a disability from being gassed by the German army. Uncle Bugg's family was very afraid of storms and used this as a storm shelter.

Equal in God's Sight

By Homer C. Ledford

After a pretty busy day in my shop
Tired and somewhat drained.
Drawn to my only window
Facing that gorgeous pine tree,
I am thinking.

An amazing thing happens.
Not one, not two, but three
Little birds alight on that pine tree limb.
One bird is black, one red, and one is brown.

How strange I think,
But then another bird joins in the lineup.
It is a white dove.
What am I seeing here?

I think, "All birds of a feather
Flock together?"
These birds are all different, but
Seem friends with each other.
What is the meaning of this?

I think, "The birds are telling me something.
Could it be we as human beings
Should see each other as all one color."
Did God create us as equals?

As the white dove left,
The others followed, all in the same direction.
Stranger still to me,
But never-the-less let's all treat each other
As God's creations. Equal.

The Letter

A letter written by Homer C. Ledford to his future wife, Colista Spradlin, dated July 4, 1952, 10:50 p.m.

At the time this letter was written, Colista was staying with her sister, Peggy Fraley, in Cincinnati, Ohio, and I was many miles away at the John C. Campbell Folk School, Brasstown, North Carolina.

Some may view this letter as romantic, some as sad, because here was a young lad about to be offered up at the altar of matrimony for the rest of his life! Some might even think it comical. I see it as very romantic and pouring my little heart out for the one I loved!

Here goes...

Thursday night —10:50

When I took your letter out of the box this afternoon, I just knew you had put some more of that fragrant smelling sachet in the letter. Darling, I appreciate things like that so much. Each little thing you do makes me so happy and proud of you.

Darling, the girl I love beats them all. Honey, I get to thinking sometimes what if I had not called you up that first night. Could I ever know what I was missing. There's no getting around it, you've meant so much to me ever since I started going with you. You've given me a new outlook on life, new hope. You've made my school days much brighter. I don't know if I could ever be any happier darling. Of course I will be after we're married. The thought of you keeps me going through the day and night. I never go to bed and get up, but what you're on my mind. I just see you in every way. When we're married (That's my favorite vision!), working for the same cause, same goal. Oh, darling I just get so full and emotional and my heart is so light and happy, I just can't find words to express myself. The only way I really can is just pull you to me and love you, love you, love you with all my heart.

It's O.K. darling if you want to write me early. Anything you do is O.K.

That $88.00 sounds pretty good. You'll be saving quite a bit pretty soon won't you? Is that $88.00 for two weeks?

Congratulations on your making an "A" on your test. You have the brains and intelligence to work with darling, but I don't. You rate an A++++ with me!!

Darling, I'm impatient. I can hardly wait until our date in Cincinnati. Keep the home fires burning. I'll see you soon.

Good night dearest. May God bless you and keep you and place his hand on you sweetheart. You're mine, and I'm yours—ALWAYS

Love you with all my heart and SOUL.

P.S. I watched a beautiful sunset tonight and darling, I was thinking about you. How God painted the sky, the clouds and painted them after you!!

LOTS OF LOVE,
HOMER

Ole Jim

By Homer C. Ledford

He wasn't my dog.
He actually belonged to my brother, Paul.
Although Paul claimed him,
Jim treasured the friendship of us all.

Paul was the one that took him hunting
which he loved almost better than eating.
But give him a big hunk of fried chicken
and he was in dog heaven.

In the wintertime when it was so cold outside
We let 'ole Jim in the house.
Stretched out in front of the nice fire,
he could dream about hunting.
It was so comforting seeing him lying there,
peaceful, not a care in the world.

Jim's color was black, but he had one
brown spot above each eye and
a heart-shaped brown spot on his chest,
An artist's design for sure.

All it took to get Ole Jim to come running
to hunt was for Paul to blow through
the shotgun barrel and here he came —
ready for to hunt squirrels, 'possums —

Time has a way of slipping by,
Memories we have — of our dogs,
people we've known,
places we've enjoyed,
churches and schools.
One thing for sure,
today, we have, yesterday's gone,
tomorrow's uncertain. Bye Jim.

The Mystery of Aunt Mary Holder

Uncle Tom Ledford had a pretty good-sized spread of farmland, a real nice white two-story house, and a two-story barn in which he could store all his bales of hay and shelter his cattle and mules. He also owned a little log cabin which set out in the lane about a half-mile from his barn. The cabin wasn't much to look at and was barely livable. The ax-hewn logs were just kinda laid on top of each other, just enough that they wouldn't fall apart. The cracks between the logs were stuffed with red clay mud, but there were plenty of cracks you could see through. There were only two rooms: the so-called living room and the back room which was used for the bedroom. They cooked in the living room!

Uncle Tom rented this cabin from time-to-time when the folks didn't have any other place to go. It was in the summer when the crops had to be tilled that Uncle Tom needed extra help, so he found this fellow by the name of Hobe Holder. Hobe's mother, Aunt Mary Holder, lived with him. Hobe wasn't married you see. Aunt Mary had reached the ripe old age of ninety-five. She had been doing pretty well until she suffered a bad heart attack and was laid to rest.

It was the custom around those parts for the local craftsman, who was usually my Uncle Bugg McDonald, to make the coffin by hand. They always had rough lumber laid back just for such as occasion. When the wooden part of the coffin was finished, the women took some nice bed sheet fabric and lined it. That was plush according to the standards of the hill country.

Now it came time to lay Mrs. Holder out in preparation for burial the next day. The women, my mother, Aunt Verlie, and Aunt Ruby, very carefully and lovingly laid out Aunt Mary in the coffin and closed the lid. Customarily, the women would "sit up" with the body all night just out of respect for the dead, I guess.

It was about midnight, the ladies were quietly sitting there, about half asleep, when a moaning sound came from the room in back. Since the door was closed between them, it was a little hard to make out what the sound was. Mother and Aunt Verlie said it sure sounded like a person groaning or gasping. Now I can tell you, Mother and the others were pretty superstitious and believed in ghosts, so they weren't about to go back there and check on Aunt Mary.

The next morning there was a lot of discussion going on about the night before and the only conclusion they could come up with was that poor Aunt Mary could have been laid out in that coffin before she was actually dead. There were no doctors or coroners in those parts to pronounce death — so be it!

I can tell you right now, I would have been a little reluctant to have gone back in that room to check too!

The Old Sorghum Mill

You just haven't lived until you have hung around an old 'lasses mill, slurping, and licking some of the sweetest tasting stuff you ever experienced in your whole life. Especially licking it off a piece of sorghum cane that has been dipped in that rich brown foamy stuff from right out of the boiling pan.

Just about everybody for miles around there in Overton County had a sorghum mill to process the molasses for all the farmers that raised sorghum cane. My Uncle Tom was one of them.

Uncle Tom's mill was located out in his pasture just about one-fourth of a mile right behind his barn. it was easy to reach from every direction.

The old mill was not only a great place to get some real good sweets, but was so interesting to watch. it was set up on two huge blocks of oak wood and the base of the mill was spiked down with railroad spikes to prevent it from tilting over since it was prone to be top heavy. There were three large rollers mounted vertically, which served to crush the cane, thus producing the juice. One of the rollers was attached to a large ten-foot beam to which the mule was hitched in order to make them go around.

Uncle Tom owned two good well-fed mules that were used to furnish the power, but only one was used at a time. He, Ole Jake or Ole Henry, was hitched up from behind to pull, but a smaller pole was inserted in the other end of the beam onto which the bridle rein was attached to make sure the mule went in a circle. Interestingly enough, that old mule would go 'round and 'round for hours until you commanded him to stop. Sometimes I would sit there on a stump nearby and watch him switch his tail, point those ears straight ahead,

I loved sorghum making time. We used a mill similar to this one used in a demonstation at Renfro Valley, Kentucky.

sometimes slinging his head as if to scare the flies off. He never seemed to be concerned too much, and I thought that was good.

The sorghum was boiled in a big four-by-eight foot pan about six inches deep and was divided into about six different compartments. The different compartments were necessary because the molasses would cook in stages, depending on the heat at the end of the pan. Of course that had a big fire built up under the cooking pan with wood to feed the fire which was rough slabs from a local saw mill. Seemed like everything fit together just fine.

It was fun to watch the men stir that beautiful amber brown syrup. To see the big bubbles come up producing what looked like steam or fog. And man, you could feel those taste buds just rising up and hollering, "Hi, Yo Silver!"

When the 'lasses were done, someone would pull up the little trap door in the drain spout and catch it all in either gallon lard buckets, or sometimes when they had so much they would use the larger fifty-pound lard cans.

When they changed "engines," Uncle Tom would take Jake loose and hitch up Ole Henry. I do believe I saw Ole Jake shake his head up and down as if to say, "Thank goodness that's over for a while!"

When school was out, instead of going on home, I would go over by the 'lasses mill. My brother, Paul, would usually go with me. Mother and Dad didn't care, especially if they didn't know it. They figured we were just playing along the old road having a good time with the other kids.

When we arrived at the mill, the first thing we did was find a good length of sorghum cane, dip it in the boiling pan where they cooked that heavenly sweet stuff, and start licking and slurping until it was running all the way down our overalls to our bare feet. Sticky, I'd reckon! Sometimes I would have a tendency to get too close to the pan where the fellows were throwing off the skimming, more like foam I guess, and I would step in the hot stuff. Boy, it didn't take me long to get my feet out of that! Mother kept telling me to wear my old brogans when I went to the 'lasses mill, but who listens to your mother when you are only ten-years-old?

A little happening that had an indelible marking on my mind was when someone's old big black dog came running up toward Ole Jake and "spooked" him pretty bad, enough to cause him to lunge sideways, break his hitching chain and take off toward the barn just "burning the wind." I have never seen a mule go so fast. Uncle Tom took off after him, couldn't run that fast mind you, but I'd say it was in high gear for Uncle Tom! Now he wore overalls that were about three sizes too large for him, and being on the skinny side, he would take three steps before his britches would catch up with him. What a sight!

After a while, here came Uncle Tom with Ole Jake and this mule was as wall-eyed as a trumped-on toad! I don't think Jake was out of his scared mood yet.

Anyway, Jake was hitched back up, and 'lasses making was back in session. I had my fill of molasses "suckers," the sun was easing down, just about ready to drop down behind Uncle Tom's old barn, and I scatted on home, eager for another day at the Old Sorghum Mill.

I occasionally play the "Hog-Lot Fiddle" during my individual shows.

Making My First Musical Instruments

E ver since I can remember, I have always wanted to play music-There was music all around me — radio, church, singing schools, family gatherings, and with all that exposure, I was bound to be drawn to it in a very big way.

My biggest handicap in learning to play any of the musical instruments found around in my area of the mountains, was I didn't have money to buy them. So being handy with a pocket knife and other woodworking tools such as coping saws, hand (carpenter) saws, chisels and the like, and pictures from Sears catalog, I set out to make my own.

My first effort was a makeshift banjo using mother's old discarded cooking pan for the body and galvanized screen wire strands from mothers window screens (she didn't know I did this until too late!) to use for strings. There were no regular banjo strings available around there at the time. I was only twelve years of age and that simple little "banjo" served the purpose very well.

The next project I tackled was a "match stick" fiddle. I had seen one a friend had made, and it just "set me on fire." I had to try my hand at that! I didn't think I could make the top and back of match sticks, but I found some old dynamite box pine material and made them from it. To avoid bending the sides, I used match sticks which I glued together vertically around the edge of the fiddle. That worked out fine, although it looked a little strange. I used a piece of Dad's stove wood for the neck, finger board, pegs and tailpiece. A nice piece of thin beech formed the bridge. A friend gave me some old used strings to complete the project. Tuned up to the proper pitch (some neighbor boys taught me the right tuning), and getting my "wanting to out ahead of everything else," I "flogged" in on it and was ready for square dancing and "THE GRAND OLE OPRY!" That is, after I learned more on how to play it-which wasn't immediately. I hasten to add! As time went on, I became less satisfied with my "creations."

By the time I had reached the ripe old age of fifteen, I wanted to make another fiddle. I had learned considerably more about instrument building by then. Sears catalog was a good source to use because they had included large pictures, the features of the instrument, and the woods used. I determined from reading Sears specifications that the wood was to be curly maple for all but the top and it was spruce.

After searching around over the place, I found a huge maple tree growing in Dad's hog-lot. Measuring over three feet in diameter. Wow! It was curly maple alright!

A very interesting story about the base of the tree was it had rotted out creating a large hollow. It was so big that Dad made a bed in it for the old sow to sleep in and have her litter of pigs.

With Dad's old dull chopping axe, I chopped out a hunk of wood big enough for the back of the fiddle, neck, tailpiece and pegs. I used a piece of dynamite box pine for the sounding board, or top.

Carving the top and back was accomplished by using a "gouge" chisel I had fashioned from a "half round" file, broken window glass to scrape with, and some sandpaper donated by my Uncle Bugg McDonald. I used my special pocket-knife that mother gave me for Christmas for carving the neck, pegs, tailpiece and bridge. I bent the sides from some maple I found in Dad's "stove wood" pile. A brushing type, brown- colored varnish finished it off. I still have that "prized" fiddle and play it in all my musical shows. I call it my HOG-LOT FIDDLE!

After four or five years had passed, I kind of lost interest in the fiddle and couldn't play very well anyway. Since there were no frets on the fiddle like are found on the mandolin and guitar, it became quite a challenge to me. The bow was another obstacle I just couldn't seem to master either. The mandolin pick seemed to fit my fingers much better so I began to look around for something easier.

Well, my older brother Paul, a little older than me, decided to purchase a mandolin from Montgomery Ward catalog and when it came, we were very surprised and disappointed because it was so small. We thought it ought to be the same size as a guitar. We had never seen a mandolin before. Paul didn't have any interest in the mandolin, so he turned it over to me and I took it from there.

I really took to the mandolin, remembering how pretty it sounded in the hands of the famous Grand Ole Opry star, Mr. Bill Monroe, who also developed the very popular Bluegrass music style we know so well today. So Paul began to learn how to play the guitar and finally we were able to play well enough to entertain at square dances and neighborhood gatherings.

'Twasn't long though, before I concluded I needed a better mandolin and decided to try to make one myself. Mother had purchased a picture of Bill Monroe from the Grand Ole Opry showing his mandolin up close. Bill's mandolin was a very complicated design and was very hard to figure out how to build. I thought long and hard on how to lay out the pattern, cut the wood, and in general get the thing all together. I would lay awake at night trying to figure it all out. Finally, I came to terms with it and after about three months, it looked like a mandolin and was ready for the finish.

I wanted to finish my very special instrument with lacquer, which I had read about in a magazine how good it was, and especially how fast the drying process was. However, the fact that it dried so fast presented a problem. You couldn't brush it on as you do varnish.

I had heard about a friend, Eugene McDonald, who had sprayed the dashboard of his car with lacquer using a common "fly sprayer," the kind you put the spray in and pump for dear life! So I decided to try that method on my mandolin-and it worked! I polished the finish with pumice stone and rotten stone to a mirror finish. I love the tone and treasure it still!

In 1946, I attended the John C. Campbell Folk School,

Brasstown, North Carolina, and learned about the mountain dulcimer. While I was there, an order came from a craft shop in New York City for two dulcimers, thinking someone there could make them for the shop. There were two customers wanting to purchase one. They had seen Jean Ritchie who was teaching at the Russell Sage Foundation School at the time and was do-

ing a lot of dulcimer playing and singing.

Of course that stirred up a lot of interest in the folk music and dulcimers. Since I had repaired a couple of old ones, I knew how they were constructed. I ended up taking on the task and made the two, which took me about two weeks. While I was working on them the folks at the school became real interested in purchasing one also. So, the first thing I knew, I was making eight dulcimers. I have been making them ever since. At present count I have made and sold nearly 6000 of those rascals!

In more recent years, I have made some real fancy instruments such as guitars, banjos, fiddles, autoharps and mandolins, I have produced thirty-six guitars, over five hundred banjos, four fiddles including the HOG-LOT FIDDLE, one autoharp, and thirty-six mandolins. Oh, yes, I invented the Dulcitar, a combination guitar and dulcimer; the Dulcibro, a dulcimer-Dobro guitar combination, and the dulcijo, a dulcimer-banjo combination. The fretless dulcimer, the dulcitar and the fretless banjo are on exhibit in the Smithsonian Institution. My custom mandolin was exhibited in the Hunter Museum, Chattanooga, Tenneesee for eight weeks. It took top honors.

I might mention that I also developed a dulcimer which is played with a violin bow instead of using a plectrum pick.

It is of special curly maple and has "the old man of the mountains" head carved on the peg box. Another instrument, dulcimer type, is the "fretless" dulcimer. Instead of frets similar to a guitar, the fingerboard is smooth, the same as a fiddle. Only inlaid fret markers are there to show where the notes are. I used some cherry wood that is over 200-years-old which helps to make the instrument look much older.

Another very special instrument is my number 5000 dulcimer. Made of all natural curly maple with a natural spruce top. The top is inlaid all around the edge with abalone shell. The body has three parts, the two outer parts resemble wings spreading away from the main body. It has a round sound hole near the back and a bridge that the strings are anchored to resembling a guitar set-up. A likeness of my head is carved on the peg box. The carving, and some of the pearl inlay was required by the owner.

At the present time, I am still making instruments and enjoying every minute of it!

At left is Jim Hawk who received my 5000th dulcimer as a gift from his wife, Mildred.

Uncle Tom had a real nice house for that neck of the woods.

My "Enterprising" Uncle Tom Ledford

D ad's brother, Uncle Tom Ledford, lived up on the hill just above the old rough wagon road that wound it's way for four or five miles up to the Black Hollow not far from where we lived just across the creek.

Overton County finally found enough money to bring an old beat-up bulldozer in and grade the road making it passable for the "Model-T" cars. There weren't many of the old Model-T's around, but they could come in our way when they wanted to, that is if the road was dry. However, when the rains came it was next to impossible for the old cars to make it through there.

Uncle Tom was not the kind to let just anything go by without noticing it. In fact, he would see just about all the cars that came by his house. If he didn't see them himself, Aunt Verlie would tell him all about it. Seeing one of those cars come by was kinda like us seeing an airplane go over-head. There just wasn't that many, you know.

One day he got to thinking on it and came up with an idea. There just might be a way to make a little much needed money for the family. He thought if he could make his own mud holes that he could cause those Model-T's to get stuck and he could bring his team of mules down and pull them out for a fee and do them a favor there, don't you see.

Tom had one of the finest teams of well fed, slick-looking, sharp-eyed mules in the country and was he proud of them. He decorated them out with the finest leather harness, the collars to go around their necks of the best soft material to be had, and the hames were topped off with the prettiest brass knobs you ever saw. They were so polished, you could look in them and pretty nigh comb your hair. The mules, named Bill and Frank, were so muscled up that I guess if you rated them it would be over 150 horse power.

Well, this one day, Uncle Tom got "wind" that there was someone headed up that way from Livingston, Tennessee, and would be there in about an hour. So he grabbed his buckets and started carrying water from his spring which was near the road, and poured it right in those holes in the road. Of course it took a few trips, but he accomplished what he had set out to do. He filled all of those holes up with water and made his own mudholes. Now he was ready for action.

Here came the old Model-T, and sure enough it got stuck on that steep hill. Tom was ready for him and down he came with his mules, hitched them up and with a good hard pull, out came the car all ready to go. Tom collected a goodly sum of "greenbacks" and seemed very pleased.

He repeated this operation from time to time and relieved those folks of enough money to buy him a new mowing machine. Not bad, not bad at all for an ENTERPRISING young feller such as my Uncle Tom.

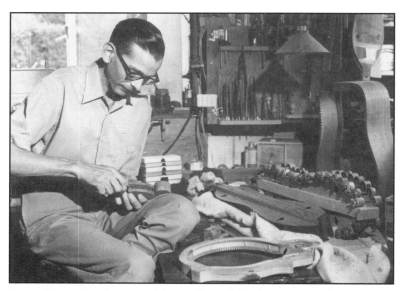

I spend countless hours making and repairing instruments in my basement workshop in Winchester, Kentucky.

Uncle Bugg's Chicken Thieves

Take the little wagon road from our house, down a little hill, across the creek, around the pasture fence for about one quarter of a mile to the "main" dirt road and there it was-Uncle Bugg's house, sitting right above the road and very handy for travelers to come in and sit a spell on his front porch, if that was the thing that was on their minds at the time, However, being situated near the road like that, also made it very handy for chicken thieves.

There weren't many folks around there that would steal chickens, or anything else for that matter. However, there happened to be one close by because Uncle Bugg was losing chickens and he just wasn't eating that many himself. This went on for a month or two, losing a fine pullet now and then. There were too many thefts to ignore for sure.

Uncle Bugg decided to put a stop to all this thievery and developed a plan. He had served in World War I and while there, learned to shoot a gun real well. Why, he could strike a match with his rifle one hundred feet away. So, what he did, he loaded his sixteen-gauge shotgun and made ready for the thieves. His bedroom faced his chicken house so when night came he parked himself at the open bedroom window. It was in the Summer

It was about midnight, or later maybe, and things began to happen. He heard the chickens squall and right then he knew he was going to be minus some chickens if he didn't make his move. About the third big squall, he leveled his old trusty sixteen-guage, cocked the hammer back, took aim, and pulled the trigger. KA-BOOM! Now to say the least, Aunt Virgie let out a scream you could hear almost across Overton County. I don't think she fully realized what Uncle Bugg was doing. Her ears were ringing like Christmas bells and she was shaking like a leaf. "Buggie, (She called him Buggie when she was excited or wanted him to come home from the field), Buggie, what happened?"

Bugg said, "Oh shut up and go back to bed. I think I have just rousted a chicken thief or two.

It so happens, the next morning Uncle Bugg went out to the chicken house to check on things, and sure enough he discovered something that looked a lot like-you guessed it, blood!

We don't know to this day exactly what happened, but one thing for sure, his chicken count was just fine from then on.

I allow as how I would have to think pretty hard on making a decision to face the old sixteen-gauge again! Wouldn't you?

When Colista and I were married in 1952, her mother wasn't sure anyone as skinny as me could make a good enough living to support a wife. Colista's dress was a bargain and I wore a borrowed suit, but I had a $100 in my pocket. Our daughter, Cindy, was married in the same dress.

Making Old Fashioned Soap in "The Good Ole Days"

We never know what each new day will bring, do we? Sometimes it's good, sometimes bad—sometimes both.

I happened to have a problem with my chassis (body) and my doctor felt obliged to send me over to his favorite hangout, the hospital, for some tests (I always have to study very hard for them in order to pass, you know). Down I went from the third floor of the parking garage, one-half block to the check-in desk, two stories up and to my final little cubicle where I checked in with the nurse who was instructed to do whatever they were instructed to do.

After getting properly checked in at the desk, I was told to go over across the hall and have a seat in the little waiting room. This I did. Some time had passed and I was getting a little bored with reading the same outdated magazines, so I began looking around for some other entertainment. You see, I had four long hours to wait and I needed something bad like!

I'll have you know, just when I thought it was going to be a long day, a couple of well dressed gentlemen came in and immediately started talking real friendly. They got into some very interesting stuff like one fellow (I'll call him Ben.), told me he had fourteen children and was raised on a farm similar to how I was brought up. We just went from one story to another, never pausing in between. We talked about chickens, hogs, haystacks, creeks, one-room schools, and all kinds of stuff you might expect a farm boy to experience.

I threw in a few stories of my own. Ben just happened to bring up the subject of bathing every Saturday night in a wash tub and using some skin- burning, hog- killing, hand-made lye soap. Now that brought me to the subject of making home-made soap the old way with caustic lye .

I remember well how Grandma and Mother used to make their own soap. It was a fairly simple process. The proper ingredients were always available around there such as old pork scraps, old lard rendered from the hog fat, and some salt, water, and caustic lye. And of course we had the old black boiling pot that we also used to boil the dirty clothes in.

The caustic lye had to be made from scratch. Mother would find an old wooden whiskey barrel, which was easily found around the community, especially up the Black Hollow. She would take plain wood ashes and pour in the barrel until it was almost full. She bored a small hole at the bottom of the barrel and inserted a small spout providing an outlet for the lye as it was made. She would pour about two gallons of water over the ashes and leave it for a couple of days, making sure the ashes were saturated well. After two more days, she would pour another two gallons of water in there and wait another day or two and boy, here it came. The prettiest dark amber- colored caustic lye you ever laid eyes on. This one process would deliver about one whole gallon of lye, enough for a lot of soap. Now everything was ready for soap making.

The fire was built under the kettle. Water, meat scraps, salt or whatever was added and then the lye was poured. As I remember, it took two pints of lye to do the job. The whole concoction was boiled until the mixture was all melted together. Of course the lye ate everything up making a nice syrupy looking compound. When Mother thought the soap was cooked long enough, she would take a tablespoon full out and drop it in cold water. If the test soap became hard in the water, it was done. After determining it to be well-cooked, she would leave the whole mess to cool and settle overnight. She would then take a large butcher knife and cut into about 2X3X5 inch cakes. Now with the soap all ready, it was time to wash all the dirty clothes that Dad, my two brothers and I had worn out on the farm all week.

About the time I finished this story, the two fellows said they would have to go and sell some medicine, and the nurse yelled for me to come on in. I guess she needed to run those tests to see if my chassis was kajuberatin right!

A Tribute to Dad

By Mattie Lee Conkwright

Mattie Lee Conkwright

A little girl with short brown hair
and a plastic doll;
A father with big strong hands
and ever so tall.

"Daddy, will you play with me?"
the little girl asks
while her father
works at his many tasks.

"Of course," he replies.
"Is your baby okay?"
And before she knows it,
her father gives up his day to play.

Walking hand in hand
down the street,
the little girl bounces her feet.
Feeling his guidance and his love,
she smiles and feels blessed from above.

Time Passages

By Cindy Lowy

The clock strikes, time falls away
Suddenly we stand in the past.
Those bittersweet memories seem so real.
How we wish we could make them last.

Another chime from the mantle clock
Brings us quickly back.
This is a day we must not waste
For it too will soon be past.

The clock chimes again as time marches on.
The future seems far away.
But even before we can turn around,
Tomorrow becomes today.

Time is no enemy if we use it well
We need not rush or linger,
The present is a gift we give ourselves,
And the past a story to remember.

Posing for a photo during a visit with my cousin, Nannie Mae, at her home in Livingston, Tennessee are from left Cindy, Nannie Mae, Mark, me and Colista.

The Old Fishing Hole

It was in the spring as I remember, about the first of May, and things were really looking up. It had just come a nice soaking rain making it too wet to work in the fields. So here came Uncle Otis sauntering up the four old plank steps to the porch to join me on my porch swing where I had already been doing a lot of thinking about what a perfect time it was to go fishing. The sun was out, no breeze to speak of, the birds were singing and the little red "fishing hook worms" were crawling all over the place!

After enjoying a few minutes of swinging, the conversation began something like this:

"Uncle Otis, you know that fishing hole down at the river just below the swinging bridge has got to be just right for us to go down and drown a few worms." "Homer, you ain't just whistling Dixie, what ya' say, lets go. I was thinking on that as I was coming up the walk there. I don't have another thing to do today. Mammy is all squared away with her ginning and knitting, so I say, okay, time's a wasting!"

So we grabbed an old tin can, scared us up a good sharp hoe, headed for the worm- rich soil in the garden and filled that can almost to the top with the juiciest red worms you ever saw.

The river and fishing hole were not very far, but we had to go out just past the barn, head straight over the hill for about one- fourth a mile, over some big rocks jutting out in the path, cross two barbed wire fences, a little creek, and walk down to the river bank and we were there.

There it was — the ole fishing hole just daring us to throw our fishing lines in!

"Homer, we're gonna have to cut us some poles to put

our lines on and I know just the place to get them. Right up here are some real nice long bambo poles that'll fit our purpose just fine."

"Yep, you're right, Otis, here's my knife—good and sharp too!"

We cut our poles, attached our lines and hooks just right, threaded on a nice juicy worm and threw those lines in with great expectations.

We sat there for awhile just being real quiet, thinking, day dreaming—I don't know what Uncle Otis was thinking about, but I had several things running through my mind—like—any minute I will catch a big prize, maybe a twelve or fourteen- inch cat, get a date with that pretty little girl that lives just aross the creek from us, play my guitar and I don't know what all.

All of a sudden, the spell was broken. Uncle Otis yelled, "I've got one, I've got one! Bring me my gloves and fish sack." You see, catfish have big ole sharp spikes sticking out from their heads and can inflict a very severe puncture wound in your hand if you don't have leather gloveson.

I grabbed the gloves and sack and delivered them to Uncle Otis and both of us managed to disengage that nice eight- pound blue cat and throw him in the sack. Boy, what a time — CATFISH FOR SUPPER! I can taste it now!

In the meantime, my line had accidently been left in the water due to all the excitement and doggone it if I didn't get to it just before it was being pulled into the water, pole and all. I grabbed the pole and started pulling for dear life. Whatever was on my hook was really "cutting a rusty." It was going every which way. I finally dug my feet in good and solid, made a final pole-breaking pull and out it came!

I yelled, "Otis, come here quick. I've got one, but in all my 'putting together,' I have never seen a fish like this. What do you think it is?"

"Homer, that is no fish. It's an eel. We're gonna have to be careful boy, look at those teeth. They'll rip you apart!"

Finally Ole Otis set his big size twelve brogan shoe down on the thing and managed to cut it loose. Then he relieved it of the responsibility of living and that was that!

Since Uncle Otis had caught his big "cat" and would have enough for his supper and mine, and because of my eel scare, I lost all interest in the fishing trip. So we put behind us the view of the old swinging bridge and the leafed-out trees along the edge of the ole fishing hole swaying to the rhythm of the rippling water flowing around the big round rocks below, and called it a day.

My nephew, Douglas McDonald, still fishes in the ole fishin' hole below our homeplace.

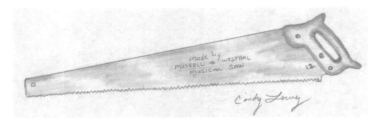

The Musical Saw

The musical saw. A MUSICAL SAW? You thought a hand saw was used for cutting wood. Well, it is but it is used for other purposes such as cutting "chunk" hamburger, slicing ham, cutting plastic laminates, and, yes, of all things, playing music — "classical music" no less!

The musical saw looks exactly like the standard hand saw; length, size of handle, number of teeth, but there is a difference. It is made of the finest English steel. I call it "spring" steel. It is cut with the grain of the steel, in other words, the saw pattern is laid out on the steel with the grain of the steel running lengthwise. I didn't realize this before, but the steel is produced at the mill by running it through large rollers to press it into sheets. It comes off the rollers much like a big roll of paper, so the grain runs with the length of the steel. So cutting the saw with the grain makes sure the vibrations of the saw are true and run lengthwise with it. This in turn produces true notes when played. Most standard handsaws used for carpentry are not cut true to grain and will not produce a good tone. Some will, but one would have to search a while to find such a saw.

I mentioned "classical" saw music above. Well, that is for real. I know of recordings of some of the classics being performed on musical saw with organ accompaniment—beautiful music! There are musical saw conventions held in California annually)and they have a "cutting up" good time I am told. You might want to give it a try. The worst you could do would be to run all your neighbors off.

My first interest in the musical saw came when I observed a friend, Mr. Asa Martin from Irvine, Kentucky, play the saw with his Kentucky Mountain Rangers several years ago. It took me some time to catch on to what was happening, but I finally discovered the "trick" He was holding the saw handle between his knees, bending downward on the main part of the saw near the handle and bending upward at the tip, thus creating an "S" shape into the blade. Another main trick was that he would follow the notes of the saw by moving the bowing away from the handle or toward it, insuring that the bowing was exactly where the notes or vibrations were. He used a fiddle bow to pull at a right angle across the back of the saw to produce the tone. When I finally mastered the technique, I was on my way.

My Cabin Creek Band, consisting of Rollie Carpenter, L.C. Johnson, Pam Case and Marvin Carroll, plays good ole time bluegrass music and has a wonderful time traveling around entertaining folks all over the world. Our music involves the standard flat top guitar, upright bass, five-string banjo, fiddle, good ole harmony singing, and my playing the mandolin, autoharp, fiddlefone, a novel instrument which I invented, and of all things—The MUSICAL SAW!

The musical saw has taken us to some mighty nice places and situations. We were priviledged to get to go to Ireland three different times to play in their *International Bluegrass Festival*. The last time we went, I took my musical saw thinking it would make a big "swath" over there and we could get a lot of publicity nationally, don't you see.

Well, we checked all our instruments at the airport, including my saw and everything seemed to be hunky dory, and they were at the time. Hold on, you know when we landed in Dublin and started to grabbing our luggage off the "merry go 'round," there was no saw to be found. Boy, I thought it had "cut" it's way out of jail and escaped! I went to, whatever they called it, the lost and found department, filled out a bale of papers and was told to be patient and it would show up and they would bring it to me.

I said, "Be sure to get it to me 'cause I have to play that thing in concert".

They said, "We will get it to you or else."

Uh-oh, I was afraid of that "or else" partly because I had heard of things like this happening before. To make a longer story short, I never did receive the saw. We did our concerts without it, had a good time otherwise and returned to the states.

About two weeks later, I was in my shop and there came a call on my phone. I slapped that phone to my ear and this is what I heard:

"Is this Mr. Homer C. Ledford?"

I said, "Yes, this is Homer Ledford."

"Well, this is Air France and we think we have a piece of your luggage, can you describe it?" "Yes, I can. This is what it looks like." "Yes, we have it and we'll get it back to you in a few days on Delta Airlines." I said, "Fine."

Right here folks, a question came across my mind. What in the world is my saw doing on the Air France lines when it went over on the Aer Lingus Airline, which is Irish? High tech is amazing, isn't it?

Another week had passed and I was in my same shop, and don't you know, a fellow from Fed-Ex came bouncing in with that piece of lost luggage—My MUSICAL SAW! I sure was glad to see that thing. It had become like a member of the family. I didn't want to make too many "cutting" remarks though, because I really did appreciate the fellow bringing it back to me. I looked at all the tags they had attached to it and found it had been through the Kennedy Airport security twice, to Jamaica once, and no telling where all else. I'm going to go on record as saying: " That saw really SAW the world!"

Memories

We all have our memories, some good, some bad. Of course we don't like to think about the bad ones—just the good ones. The good ones makes us feel good—takes us back to other times in the past. Sometimes we like to tell them to someone else. As a matter of fact, just today a guitar customer came into my shop and started talking. I could see he was a big talker and the friendly type so I started to talking too. We just opened up our souls, so to speak.

We started talking about things that happened to us in our childhood. He said he was brought up just like me— didn't have much. I liked that. We had so much in common to talk about that we just completely forgot about guitars, don't you know.

My customer kept pulling at me to tell him about some of the things that happened to me and I felt obliged to do so.

I told him about one of my special memories of sitting on the front porch at home there on top of the river hill. It was late in the evening close to sundown, but I could still see the rugged mountains rising up toward the sky. I wondered a lot about those mountains. What was beyond? Were there people living over there? Could there be big black bears, foxes, coons, or whatever? A twelve-year-old kid like me could let his imagination run away with him you know.

The very next day, Mother came up to me and asked if I would like to have her collection of old eyeglass lenses, and I said, "Yeah, I would."

I got to thinking what I could do with those magic things. All of a sudden it occurred to me, when you looked through them it would make things look bigger. Well I found me a cardboard tube such as paper towels are rolled on and spaced those lenses inside of it, and lo and behold, I had me a telescope. I focused my telescope on those mountains and man I could see the birds, buzzards, and hawks a flyin' all over the place. I could even see Dad milking the cow down at the barn, pulling on those teats and forcing out the prettiest white stream of milk you most ever saw!

When Mother discovered what I had done, she bragged on me something wonderful. She said I was a genius to think all that up and that she felt real proud of me. That did make me feel real good, and I thought that maybe some of it could be true.

My guitar customer thought he would like to tell a story long about now, so of course I let him. His story reminded me of another so he wondered if I would relate something else. Yes, I thought I could.

This one you won't believe, but I have to tell it anyway. I guarantee it is the truth.

We had heard about airplanes but had never seen or heard one. We didn't even know the size of one and really didn't believe there was such a thing that you could fly in. No siree! Well, I want to tell you what happened that day. Mother, Dad and I were out in the garden cutting weeds out of the vegetables and there came a sound we had never heard before. It just kept getting closer and closer, and buddy we threw those hoes down and looked skyward and there it was. From my Uncle Bugg's description, it was an airplane alright. Now comes the big excitement. That plane was not only going across our pasture, but real low 'til you could see the fellow in it. It just kept getting lower, and lower until it disappeared over the hill above our house. We just knew that plane had crashed so we took off up the hill to see, and sure enough there it was sitting right in the middle of Uncle Otis's corn field! I just don't know how the pilot managed to get it down without crashing, but he did.

We rushed up to the plane and by this time the pilot was getting out. We did our usual howdy's and stuff and asked him how come he landed here in the corn field. He explained he had lost his map and was following the West Fork river to get him to Jamestown, Tennessee, and that if he could successtully land, he could ask someone directions. Somehow, Dad thought that didn't make good sense. Mother thought he was crazy. Maybe she didn't miss it too much judging from what he had just done.

We asked him how in the world was he going to get that contraption back in the air. He said it would be simple. You could take off or land this Piper Cub on a dime and get back nine cents in change! Well, I had my doubts about that but I thought we would see.

He jumped back in the plane, got it started, and revved up the engine real good, making that propeller spin 'til you couldn't see it. The next thing we knew that plane seemed to jump almost straight up and off he went. It took down about fifTy good feet of Uncle Otis's corn, but I guess that was okay. We never did tell him what had happened to it.

After that story, my guitar buddy allowed as how he had a couple more things he would like to relate. First thing I knew he got off on the subject of trains and that reminded me of a train story.

As I've said before, the West Fork River wound its way down just below our barn—straight over the hill. It was situated right down in the deep valleys formed by the mountains around. When the wind blew just right, it brought strange sounds with it. You could hear the cows lowing, chickens cackling, women hollering for their husbands to come eat supper, and yes, the beautiful sounds and wails of the coal trains up the river in the little coal town of Wilder. Wilder was a good name for it because it sure was a "wild" place, especially on Saturday nights when some of the natives would get drunk and have their weekly shoot-outs.

Mom and Dad and us four kids would wonder what a train looked like. Dad suggested maybe it was some kind of car. I pictured in my mind a bunch of trucks hitched together, which later proved I wasn't too far off. I thought the whistle we heard was someone blowing through something like a huge metal horn shaped like a funnel. I sure wanted to see one real bad. It wasn't long until I had my chance.

My uncle, Harris McDonald, lived on the Cumberland

Plateau in the Clarkrange Community and one day my two cousins Lois and Leslie, Uncle Harris's children, wanted me to come out and visit and see their new house Uncle Harris had built. I wanted to go real bad, but I realized I had no way to go the thirty miles except to walk and I wasn't about to do that. Mother and Dad wouldn't have let me anyway.

We got to checking and found out the mail truck for the area went all the way up State Route 85 almost to Uncle Harris's house. Also, the route took it through the little coal towns of Wilder and Crawford where they said the trains were. I began to beg Mother to let me ride the mail truck and visit my cousins, and she finally let me go. Mother knew the dangers of going through Wilder so she warned me to be sure not to get off the truck while I was there. I heeded Mother's warning and didn't dare get off that truck. I was too scared to. I could imagine everyone around there carrying guns who would shoot at the drop of a hat.

Well, the biggie happened. Just as we left Wilder my ears were just about knocked out by the loudest scream I had ever heard. Here it came, an honest to goodness TRAIN. It was the longest thing I had ever seen. I think it was two miles long, and all the cars were loaded to the top with big black chunks of coal. It was a thrill to see the big engine laboring to pull all of that. It seemed like it was having a hard time because the giant plumes of black smoke rolled out of that thing in puffs, as if it was getting its breath real hard. That part bothered me a little. I didn't want to see *anything* work that hard.

Well, I finally got to see the train whose whistle we had heard coming down the valley defined by the West Fork River. You know, education is wherever you can find it, isn't it?

Long about now it was time to stop story-telling because my guitar buddy and I had run out of stories and my wife Colista was buzzing the intercom for me to come and eat. I knew better than to aggravate her any, so I headed upstairs right now for some of her fine cooking! Anyway, story-telling always makes me hungry.

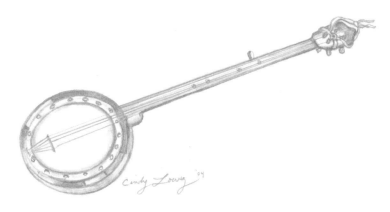

Uncle Caleb's Banjo

By Homer C. Ledford

It always hung right behind
the old hand- hewn door
leading into the bedroom.
Uncle Caleb 's banjo

An old groundhog leather string
wound around the tuning pegs
and hooked on a nail driven
in the wall kept it secured.

Uncle Caleb was mighty proud
of that old instrument with the old skin head
made of groundhog hide and
with only sixteen brackets
to keep the head tight.

It didn't matter with him though,
just as long as it made that sweet ringing sound.
He didn't profess to be a singer
but could bring his big knuckled fingers
down across those five strings,
making them sing —
ringing over those hills —
challenging the prettiest songs of the little birds
sitting on the tree limbs listening, singing.

Continued

Sitting on the porch of the little cabin on the hill,
just above the little creek snaking its way
down it's troubled path leading to the river,
strumming that old banjo and unknown
to him, cousin Charles and myself,
listening to the strains of Cripple Creek, Old Joe
Clark, and tapping out the beat with his much
worn "brogan" shoes.

Uncle Caleb — pickin', thumping, whistling —
Feeling the wind that blows across
those trees that grew out over the hills,
huge beech, oaks, maples, bowing down
as if to sway to the rhythm of his special kind of
music.

Charles and me, just across the creek
perched on our favorite little seat on the rock
jutting out from the hillside
hanging on to every note.

Little did Uncle Caleb know
that he was teaching me to play
the banjo the old claw-hammer way,
 the only one found in the hill country in those days.
One day, I surely will own an old banjo
like Uncle Caleb's.

Years pass, memories burned in my consciousness,
Old time music — banjos, fiddles, guitars,
singing, churches with spires reaching toward
    Heaven.
And, yes, I do strum an old banjo like the one
he played on back then
And ...
THANKS, UNCLE CALEB!

Wrong Doctor!
(Fictitious)

As you grow older you know things begin to happen to you like you lose your appendix, your teeth, joints wear out, the battery in your brain begins to read minus instead of plus and I don't know what all! Why, I can tell you right now I am traveling some rough road. My frame is becoming warped. I'm pulling eighteen degrees off plumb!

Ole Arthritis and all his kinfolk have attacked and my joints are feeling like two pieces of sandpaper rubbing together. Some of my more active joints are beginning to lock up on me, if you know what I mean.

Well, I decided to go the doctor and see what could be done. Some friends highly recommended Dr. D.M. Bhonus. I thought that would be copacetic since he specialized in bone and frame problems. So, I got me an appointment and went! I dragged myself up the steps and into the waiting room and was met by the receptionist who immediately asked, "What brings you here today sir?

I replied, "Mainly strength and awkwardness."

"Is this your first visit here?"

I said, "Yeah it is."

"Well here, take these forms and fill them out to the best of your knowledge."

There were only fifteen pages. My appointment was for 2:00 p.m. and I got to see the doctor at 4:00. Even though it took two hours to fill out the forms, I think I passed the test!

Finally the nurse came in and said, "Come right on in." And I did.

She said: "Sit right here in this chair." And I did. "The doctor will see you in just a jiffy." And he did!

The doctor got right to it using his most professional manner.

"Mr. Ledford, how long have you been bothered with this condition?"

"Well, it's been putting me through a lot of stress. My psyche isn't working too good either."

Doc asked, "Are you very regular, is it keeping you up a lot at night?"

"Yes, Doc, I can say I do regularly have quite a bit of pain, and it disturbs my sleep pretty much."

"This doesn't sound too good. Where is most of the pain concentrated?"

"Doc, I get a lot of discomfort when I bend my knees and also in my shoulders and neck."

"Oh, my goodness, Mr. Ledford, there's been a big mistake here. You have been directed to the wrong place. I am a doctor of urology. You need to go next door and see Dr. D.M. Bhonus, the orthopedic surgeon!"

Don't you know, I was getting a bit suspicious with all the impertinent questions and other things going on. Now, I was faced with another problem, filling out fifteen pages of those dad-blasted forms again. I think I'll just go on home. I'm not hurting nearly as bad as I was!

Here I am, ready to input something on my new computer.

Computers

Years ago, and I'm not saying how many, understand, down in the mountains of Tennessee where I grew up, we started out with the new-fangled hand cranked telephone. Then came the spring wound phonograph. The radio was next and a big hit, and boy that was a bit of "high technology." We were "cooking with steam" then!

Much later when I was attending Berea College, we began to hear about television. News was spreading all over. Television was going to be the "thing."

One of the retail stores out in the west end of Berea, was running a promotion. They were inviting the public to come in and watch the new WHAS Louisville channel. I think it was the first channel to go on the air in Kentucky. Some of my friends and I skipped gym class and went out to experience this phenomenon. They flipped that thing on and there it was, the first television I had ever seen. It was interesting, but about all I could make out was some music and a lot of "snow." Impressed? Yes, but let me tell you about what was to come down the road.

Later, I was living in Winchester, Kentucky, and owned a "hi fi" record player, a nice color television no less, radio, and three telephones. I felt like I was pretty complete along the lines of entertainment and communication. But hold it just a minute! Not quite! The big word COMPUTER began to circulate around. The first place I ever heard of a computer was in a business machines class at Berea College. So at least I was familiar with the word. More and more of my friends talked about what a great machine it was and how you could communicate with the whole world, type letters, and make all kinds of documents. The sky was the limit.

Yes, it happened. The little wheels began to turning in my brain and they calculated I might ought to get me one of those things. I looked at some prices, and wow, how in the world would I ever be able to pay for one? I would have to make more dulcimers, repair a few more instruments, and maybe even sneak back some grocery money. That was very risky though because my wife, Colista, sure kept a tight fist on that! I finally came up with the right sum and was ready buy one, but didn't know more'n a goose about what to buy.

To the rescue! My son, Mark, worked at the University of Kentucky in Lexington, programming computers and setting them back up when they "crash." He said he would go with me to help me make a selection. Also, a good friend, Mr. Bill Johnson of Lexington, found out about it and said he would go help with the purchase. I thought, "This is really 'hunky-dory,' so let's go."

After the purchase, my friend Bill said he would even come over to Winchester and set the thing up for me. How lucky can you get!

I watched him do the usual unpacking, checking out the cords, books, and warranties, and finally, he had it all hooked up and ready to throw the switch. Now, right here folks is where the trouble started. Usually the trouble starts later, but no, not for me. Wouldn't you know it, the computer wouldn't "boot up!" I reckon "boot up" means to start it up, or something close to that. Bill tried everything in the book. He called the manufacturer, the telephone company, and I don't know who all else, but he didn't call the ambulance service or police since they didn't seem to "have a dog in that fight."

Bill concluded that the computer was defective, and agreed he would take it back to the store where we bought it and exchange it for me. Yep, that's what he did. He brought the new one back and this time everything was A OK. Now we're cooking! At this point I expressed to Bill that I didn't know "beans" about how to "compute."

Bill said, "Just a simple little ole thing. Here, I'll show you."

First thing I knew, he had gone through so many of those "simple things," that I forgot what the first one was. I guess you can't feed the cow the whole bale of hay at once!

The first operation I learned to do was type on it. Since I had a good course in typing in college, I didn't have to use the "hunt and peck" system thank goodness.

I continued to pick up a little now and then, but one day, about six or eight months later, the inevitable happened. I purchased another impossible gadget to go with my computer—a scanner. I was going to print out an enlarged color picture of my lovely wife, Colista. I had everything set up according to instructions. The picture was in and I threw the switch and BLOOEY! The whole system went down and didn't even say "bye!" I was told later that my computer didn't have enough "memory." I can identify with that memory thing. Apparently the big 8X10 inch picture was too much for it to handle.

Along came my good friend Bill Johnson again and to the rescue. He put in a new—oh well, let me see—oh yeah, hard drive. I was going to say the "soft drive," but I knew that wouldn't work. Bill is so nice, he even threw in a few extra "memories." So now I was back "cooking" again.

I was going on pretty good for about another year, and I guess the moon just wasn't right because I was typing a letter to my daughter, Mattie Lee, and all of a sudden the screen (You might call it a monitor.) went graveyard dead, a real dark color of black. This time my technicians, Bill and Carleton Sculley, *both* came to my rescue. I would have tried to work on it myself, but according to Bill and Carleton, my screwdrivers, hammer, electric drill and pocket-knife weren't the proper tools. Anyway, working on a computer didn't follow along the lines of repairing a banjo, you know.

Due to my not trying to work on it and Bill's and Carleton's fantastic skills, my precious computer was back on the "well" list again. Whew!!

One day after that, I was trying to work out a document for my business and I was really trying to get fancy. I was italicizing, making some words bolder, throwing in the beautiful colors and all, and it really was going well until my little "pinky" went wild and hit the "Ctrl" key and the whole thing left the scene! Nothing, nada. I didn't know any good words right then to describe how I felt but if I did, I probably couldn't print them! No, I was never able to get it back. The best thing to do at the moment was to give it a good kick and throw the switch!! And I did!!

I had some real good times. Success was on my side for about six months, but another crash happened. Black again. I called upon a good friend and he was here in a jiffy. He took his little handy dandy screwdriver, took all thirty-five screws out of the back and unplugged things I never knew existed. He flipped through keys, programs, windows, and whatever else he could think of and thought he had it. Maybe he did, but you know what?

That little plug was the last to plug in and it looked so innocent. The receptacle was right next to the plug so my friend, thinking that was the right one, he jammed it right into place. If you thought the screen was black before, this time it was blacker! The plug was put exactly in the wrong hole! Black smoke and fumes rolled out of that thing enough to kill an elephant, and my friend's face lit up like a welding torch! He slid back in his chair and very calmly made the statement, "I guess that was the wrong hole." And I guess, no, I *know* he was right. The computer was taken to the shop and completely rebuilt.

This is approximately three months later and to the best of my knowledge my computer is experiencing several months of good health. Anyway, here I am typing this little story. It can't spell too well though!

Dr. Braininiski

(Fictitious)

Sometimes when you don't understand what a term means, it might not be good for your health and well-being!

Recently I went to see Dr. Braininski about a problem I was having. I went in and there was only one person in the waiting room ahead of me, so I concluded my mental state would be just about right for what was to come. Dr. Braininski appeared at the door and said, "Good morning, Mr. Ledford, just come right on in and let's see what the problem is."

I said, "Doc, I've been feeling so depressed lately and don't seem to function well. I just don't feel like anybody cares. Can you help me? Doc replied, "Yes, I think I can."

After temperature, blood pressure, and knee reaction tests, he pushed back in his chair and said, "Mr. Ledford, what you need is a lot of "TLC." I said, "Yes, I think you are right doc. I will go back and give it the old "Honest Abe" try!

I went home and my wife came in and saw me lying on the couch and started hollering, lamblasting, and complaining that I didn't help her wash the dishes, do the washing, or anything around the house.

You know what I did? I gave her a good tongue lashing like you never heard before and I told her where she could go, and that was that, or so I thought. When I woke up, I thought I had better get to the doctor fast. And I did!

I arrived back at Dr. Braininski's office looking mighty sad. Dr. Braininski received me back in his laboratory, turned around and took a good look at me and exclaimed, "What in the world happened to you? Why do you have that black eye and lips all swollen up like that?"

I said, "Doc, you told me I should have some TLC. I tried it and this is what happened"!

"No, Mr. Ledford, you must have misunderstood what TLC means. It means TENDER LOVING CARE."

No wonder I had the problem. I thought it meant TAKE LESS COMPLAINING.

Doctor Braininski has tried another approach since then, and so far it has almost worked. I think!

Members of Homer Ledford and the Cabin Creek Band are from left, Rollie Carpenter, Marvin Carroll, Pamela Case, Homer Ledford, and L. C. Johnson.

Going Exactly Right in the Wrong Direction

I have a bluegrass band which we call Homer Ledford and the Cabin Creek Band. It consists of five members: Pam Case, who slaps the ole upright bass something fierce and sings high tenor; Rollie Carpenter, who plays banjo and guitar and sings lead and baritone vocals; L.C. Johnson, who plays guitar and sings lead and baritone; Marvin Carroll, who saws the fiddle and occasionally plays the "claw hammer banjo," and me. I play the mandolin.

I think we have a good sound and I think that is due to the fact we are all such good friends. We travel a lot together and have a ball. We use my seven passenger van because it will hold all our instruments, P.A. system and still leave plenty of room for all of us. Pam prefers to take the back seat which is a bench seat. She just lies down back there and sleeps or reads. We call that seat "Pam's pad."

Sometimes on our trips we take a wrong turn and get lost, not real bad but bad enough to have to stop and ask directions.

We were on a trip to do a gig in a little college near Chattanooga, Tennessee, and possessed the necessary directions to get there. However, I was driving this time and went right past the sign. I am the one who argues with signs! We went about five miles out another road, the wrong one of course. Finally Pam said, "Homer, I think we are lost."

"Pam, you let me do the driving and we'll all be fine."

You see Pam had already awakened and was becoming a little vociferous, which she is capable of doing now and then.

I finally realized Pam was right. We were headed exactly right in the wrong direction!

I decided to go back and pull off at a restaurant we had just passed to see if anyone there could help us. No, not really, they said they thought we were lost though!

Pam had her little cell phone with her and whipped it out and said, "Homer, if you'll give me that dad-blamed number, I'll call the folks where we are going and they can get us there." By now we were running out of time. We needed to be there in about forty-five minutes—on stage!

Pam called and got the office right away. "We're lost," she said. "Homer made a wrong turn and can you tell us how to get there?"

"Where are you exactly? Give me the name of the road and how far out you are and I will talk you in."

"We're about five miles out and right now on Route 58, if I remember correctly."

"Well, from there you take a right turn and it will bring you right to us. Just come up the long driveway to the administration building and we will meet you."

"Fine!"

The only problem was the folks at the office misunderstood which way we were headed in the first place. Here we went, feeling good all over more than anyplace else!

We proceeded on and it seemed like forever and it felt like we ought to be there by now, for sure. All of a sudden a big sign popped up before my eyes and guess what it read, "WELCOME TO GEORGIA!" Now if that don't "beat the bugs a fightin'!" Here we were, headed exactly right in the wrong direction again!

Finally I turned around and headed in the right direction this time and we did reach our destination. I think we had about ten minutes to spare before going on stage.

I'd like to announce we did do our show in spite of the confusion and I might add—WE RECEIVED A STANDING OVATION!!

Getting Lost at Christmas

The following is a true story that happened to us, Homer Ledford and the Cabin Creek Band, on November 28, 2000.

We agreed to play for a friend's Christmas party in a very uptown subdivision in Clark County near where I live in Winchester, Kentucky. Lonnie Pendleton, whose house where we were supposed to go, gave me very good directions, and I had them all figured out to the letter. Well, it was snowing that night and I was leading the way with great confidence. Everything was going well except when it came to the street signs. The snow had covered them so that It made them impossible to read. I just proceeded on, thinking I would take the next turn. The only trouble with that decision was everything went wrong.

After going for what seemed endless miles, I came to the conclusion it was best to turn around and start back and wish for better luck. This time the signs were more legible because the snow hadn't covered the other side of them. Making the correct turn, we finally found a house that fit the right description Lonnie had given me. There were all these cars parked there, suggesting to us, boy, this is the place! It sure looked like they were having a big party all right. There were lights and huge candy canes. Man, was that some vision for my hungry eyes!

The front door was open so we took that as our big invitation and walked right on in. All ten of us. You see, there were the five of us in the band, and we had some guests with us. There were some folks near the door and so I explained that we were supposed to make some music for the party and they said, "Going to have music, eh? That's great, just come right on in. Go right on downstairs and I'm sure we'll be on down in a little while."

We went down into the basement and looked over in the corner at a huge table just loaded with some of the most delicious looking food you ever saw! Pam Case, our bass player, headed over and loaded her plate full of food. It looked like a triple-decker! Pam was starving, hadn't eaten all day.

I decided I had better go up and tell the owner, Lonnie Pendleton, that we were here and ready to start pickin'. I just happened to know one of the guests up there and asked him where Lonnie was. "Lonnie? Lonnie who?"

Uh, oh, something wrong here. We had a problem. My friend said, "You have the wrong house. If you are talking about Lonnie Pendleton, he lives down the street on the left about the fifth house."

I wasted no time getting downstairs and telling the gang. "It's all off, we've got to get out of here, and Pam, put that food back." She said, "Nothing doing, I haven't had anything to eat all day and I'm starving."

Irvine, Rollie Carpenter's brother, said, "I wonder if they have a back exit to this place?"

"Yes, here it is, lets get outta' here!" So we did and never looked back!

The owner never saw us there.

I called the owner of the place the next morning and explained to him what happened and he said, "Oh, that was OK, we just got a big kick out of it!"

We did get to Lonnie's place that night and enjoyed the party. Pam didn't eat much at Lonnie's party though!

Glossary of Appalachian Terms and Expressions

Aigs, hen fruit, cackle berries — Granny sold a settin' of aigs today.
Ailin' — Sick. Granny is ailin' today.
Ain't — Same as hain't.
Allus — Always. I allus did like chocolate pie.
Atall — At all. Pa wouldn't stand for that atall.
Atter — After. We went swimming atter school.
Betwixt — Between. He was pretty dense betwixt this ears.
Bile — Boil. Bile them cabbage down.
Borrie — Borrow. May I borrow some coal oil, Virgie?
Chawed — Chewed. The cow chawed her cud.
Cided — Decided. I cided not to go with him.
Cranky — Fussy. Ma is shore cranky today.
Crick — Creek. I'll see ye flirther up the crick!
Cuss — Curse. He shore cussed him out good!
Dang, tarnation, i-gad, e-gad — By-words. I'll be danged if I'll do it!
Druther — Rather. I'd druther not do it.
Feller — A fellow. He's the right feller for me.
Fetch — To bring. Fetch me up a pail of water.
Flivver — Car-Come take a ride in my flivver.
Flustered — Frustrated. Im too flustered to think.
Froggy — Jumpy-He was mighty froggy today.
Fur — Far. It's a fur piece to the barn.
Gawked — To stare. He gawked me like I was crazy.
Gonna — Going to. Haint you gonna stay tonight?
Hain't — Isn't or is not. "It hain't so."
Hant — Ghost. Halloween is the season for hants.
Hit — It. Hit proves I was right.
Hoss — Horse or mule. Saddle up my hoss for me.
Howdy — Hello. Howdy stranger.

Jis — Just. He drank jis a little swig.

Josh — To tease, kid. Don't josh him about her.

Larpin good — Very good. Apple pie is larpin good.

Lassie — Young girl. She's a beautil lassie.

Nary — None. There was nary a bite left for me.

No 'acount — No good. The taters were no 'acount.

Noggin — Head. His noggin is too big for his hat.

Overhalls — Overalls-My overhalls are too short.

'Peared — Appear. It 'peared like he was drunk.

Pick-a-lick, jammin' — Playing a little music. Want to go pick-a-lick on the ole guitars?

Pint —Point. Just pint it out to me.

Plum — Totally. Gramps is plum well now.

Pore — Poor. To be pore is not a sin.

Putty — Pretty. She's as purty as I've ever seen.

Pyore — Pure. That is pyore strength moonshine, allright!

Quare — Queer. He had a quare way of doing it.

Riled — Angry, aggravated. Don't git riled up over nuthin.

Rite smart — Quite a bit. He stutters a right smart.

Sartin — Certain. He is sartin to get drunk tonight.

Scraggled — Unkempt. He shore had a scraggedly beard.

Scrounge — To push in between. We scrounged right in between the two isles.

Seed — Saw. I seed him do it.

Shady — Dishonest or not to be trusted. He sure is a shady character.

Skiddish — Suspicious-I was mighty skidish of him

Snicker — Giggle, laugh. Here comes Sal with a snicker and grin.

Snucked — Sneaked. We snucked into the movie.

Some'rs — Somewhere. We are goin' out some'ers tonight.

Sorter — Sort of-He sorter had a kaniption fit.

So's — So as. Hope it rains so's I can go fishing.

Spell — A short time. Come sit a spell, Granny.

Tater — Potato. Dig them taters a row at a time.

Thang — Thing. That thang has done pooped out.

Throde — Throwed. He throwed his arm out.

Tole — Told. He sure tole him off.

Twas — It was-Twas a mighty fine game.

White lightnin', moonshine, recipe — Whiskey. I'll drink me a good shot of moonshine tonight.

Whup — Whip. Mother threatened to whup me.

Your'n — Your's. That trap is not your'n.

Mountain creeks nourish trees, flowers, and the imaginations of little boys and girls. I hope you enjoyed my recollections and have been nourished by them.

See ya' Further Up the Creek,

Homer C. Ledford

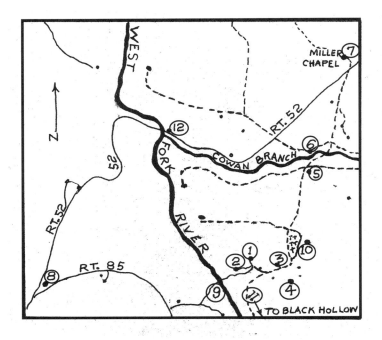

MAP LEGEND OF OVERTON COUNTY

1. Homer's home place
2. Grandpa and Grandma McDonald's cabin
3. Uncle Bugg and Aunt Virgie McDonald's home
4. Aunt Nora Todd's home
5. Uncle Tom and Aunt Verlie Ledford's home
6. The Ivy Point (Ivyton) School House
7. Miller Chapel Church
8. Uncle A.H. Copeland (Abe) and Aunt Nannie's store and home
9. The old swinging bridge below our house
10. The Ferrell Cemetary
11. The road leading up to the Black Hollow which ends at the mountain and the site of moonshine still
12. The concrete bridge across the West Fork River
13. Route 52, the black-top road from Livingston to Jamestown, Tennessee
14. West Fork River and Cowan Branch, our favorite stream to play in

Recordings by Homer Ledford

MOUNTAIN MEMORIES—CD with nineteen selections of folk music performed by Homer on several instruments he made, including the autoharp, guitar, mandolin, dulcimer, fiddle and banjo. Ruth (McLain) Smith sings five gospel selections, including: Not Good Enough by Colista Ledford, Amazing Grace, How Great Thou Art, and Christmas Memories by Homer. Homer's daughter; Julia Baker, plays violin on Edelweiss and her sister, Mattie Lee Conkwright, cello. Homer plays the musical saw on My Old Kentucky Home.

TAPES: DULCITONE—Homer features the dulcimer, but also plays the guitar, mandolin plus the dulcitar and dulcibro, two instruments he invented. The dulcitar is registered in the U.S. Patent Office and is on display in the Smithsonian Institute.

THE OLD COUNTRY CHURCH: An all gospel project of twelve selections including: Amazing Grace, How Great Thou Art, Not Good Enough, by Colista Ledford, Christmas Memories by Homer, The Old Country Church, and Angel Band, all sung by Ruth (McLain) Smith of the famous McLain Family band. The rest are instrumentals performed on instruments made by Homer.

CUTTING THE GRASS: Twelve instrumental selections with Homer playing the bass, mandolin and guitar. Selections include: Under the Double Eagle, Edelweiss, Cutting the Grass, by Homer, My Old Kentucky Home on the musical saw, and others. Homer Plays some beautiful arrangements with "twin mandolins."

Recordings by Homer Ledford and the Cabin Creek Band

THE BEST OF HOMER LEDFORD AND THE CABIN CREEK BAND: Nineteen selections including: Shady Grove, Jimmy Brown the Newsboy, The Violet and the Rose, Amazing Grace, and I'm On My Way Back to the Old Home. The band consists of Pam Case on bass and vocals, Rollie Carpenter, banjo, guitar and vocals, L.C. Johnson on guitar and vocals, Homer plays mandolin and autoharp and Marvin Carroll on fiddle.

WE MISSED YOU IN CHURCH LAST SUNDAY: fourteen bluegrass gospel selections including: We Missed You in Church Last Sunday, What a Friend, Keep on the Sunny Side of Life, I Found a Way, I heard My Mother Call My Name in Prayer, My Lord and I, and eight other favorites.

ALL TAPES: $10 each
CD'S: $15 each
Add $1.75 postage for each item.

The book: *DULCIMER MAKER, THE CRAFT OF HOMER LEDFORD,* by R. Gerald Alvey, published by THE UNIVERSITY PRESS OF KENTUCKY with foreword and afterword by Ron Pen, director of John Jacob Niles Center of American Music. This book tells how to make an Appalachian dulcimer from start to finish. To order, contact Homer at the address below. PRICE: $19.95

Homer C. Ledford, 125 Sunset Heights, Winchester, Kentucky 40391. Website: http://members.aol.com,Homer C. Ledford, 125 Sunset Heights, Winchester, Kentucky 40391. E-mail: spradel@aol.com Phone: 1-859-744-3974

HARMONY AND ME, by Cindy Lowy, published by Chicago Spectrum Press. A guide to living a more balanced, peaceful life. Cindy uses two characters, "Harmony" and "Chaos," to show how to connect with your creator and the angelic beings that guide and protect you. To order see below. PRICE: *$20.95*

Cindy Lowy, 7504 Deer View Court, Louisville, Kentucky, 40241. Web site: www.cindylowy.com
E-mail: cindylowy@aol.com Phone: l (502) 228-6130

Songs Included on Compact Disc

All the selections listed below are played on instruments Homer made with the exception of the bass and musical saw. Homer also wrote and plays all the selections with the exception of those otherwise listed.

1. **West Fork Breakdown** — Guitar, bass. Homer's "Hog-lot Fiddle"is used on this number.
2. **Edelweiss** — (Traditional). Julia Baker-violin, Mattie Conkwright-cello, Homer on mandolins, guitar and bass
3. **Cutting the Grass** — Two mandolins, guitar, bass
4. **Colista's Waltz** — Mandolin, guitar, bass. Written in honor of Homer's wife, Colista.
5. **Blackberry Blossom** — (Traditional). Mandolin as played on Michael Johnathon's *Woodsongs Old Time Radio Hour* before a live audience
6. **Wildwood Flower** — (Traditional) Dulcimer, guitar, bass
7. **Mountain Memories** — Mandolins, guitar, bass
8. **Not Good Enough** — (Colista Ledford) Vocal by Ruth (McLain) Smith
9. **Shout Ole Lou** — (Traditional) Played on the *dulcijo,* an instrument developed by Homer and played on a live broadcast of the *Woodsongs Old Time Radio Hour.*

Continued

10 0 **Shennandoah** — (Traditional) Appalachian dulcimer with guitar and mandolin

11. **Time Passages** — (Cindy Lowy) Cindy recites this poem with autoharp music in the background. The chimes heard are from the grandmother clock Homer made.

12. **Bluegrass March** — Two mandolins, guitar, bass, rhythm sticks

13. **0 Danny Boy** — (Traditional) Julia Baker-violin. Homer on mandolin, guitar, bass

14. **Christmas Memories** — Autoharp, mandolin, guitar, bass. Vocal by Ruth (McLain) Smith

15. **Mandolin Holiday** — Three mandolins, guitar, bass

Homer made the "Hog-Lot Fiddle" by looking at a picture in the Sears Roebuck catalog. The wood was cut from a huge maple tree that grew in his Dad's hog-lot, dried in his mother's wood-burning cook stove and carved out using a pocket knife his mother gave him for Christmas. He also used a gouge chisel he made from an old half-round file.

Cindy Lowy is a highly respected author, artist, speaker, and jewelry maker. She is the author of the popular book, *HARMONY AND ME.*

Julia Baker plays violin in the Lexington Philharmonic Orchestra. Ruth (McLain) Smith was a member of the famous McLain Family Band.